The Homeless Population

ISSUES

Volume 189

Series Editor

Lisa Firth

Independence

Educational Publishers

Cambridge

32544A

D0318187

First published by Independence

The Studio, High Green

Great Shelford

Cambridge CB22 5EG

England

© Independence 2010

British Library Cataloguing in Publication Data
The homeless population. -- (Issues ; v. 189)

1. Homelessness--Great Britain. 2. Homeless persons--

Services for--Great Britain.

I. Series II. Firth, Lisa.

362.5'0941-dc22

ISBN-13: 978 1 86168 540 7

Printed in Great Britain
MWL Print Group Ltd

CONTENTS

Chapter 1 Homelessness Issues

Chapter 2 Youth Homelessness

Chapter 3 Homelessness Solutions

OTHER TITLES IN THE ISSUES SERIES

For more on these titles, visit: www.independence.co.uk

EXPLORING THE ISSUES

Photocopiable study guides to accompany the above publications. Each four-page A4 guide provides a variety of discussion points and other activities to suit a wide range of ability levels and interests.

A note on critical evaluation

Because the information reprinted here is from a number of different sources, readers should bear in mind the origin of the text and whether the source is likely to have a particular bias when presenting information (just as they would if undertaking their own research). It is hoped that, as you read about the many aspects of the issues explored in this book, you will critically evaluate the information presented. It is important that you decide whether you are being presented with facts or opinions. Does the writer give a biased or an unbiased report? If an opinion is being expressed, do you agree with the writer?

The Homeless Population offers a useful starting point for those who need convenient access to information about the many issues involved. However, it is only a starting point. Following each article is a URL to the relevant organisation's website, which you may wish to visit for further information.

What is homelessness?

Information from Shelter.

Broadly speaking, the law defines somebody as being homeless if they do not have a legal right to occupy any accommodation, or if their accommodation is unsuitable to live in. This can cover a wide range of circumstances, including, but not restricted to, the following:

⇨ having no accommodation at all;

⇨ having accommodation that is not reasonable to live in, even in the short-term (e.g. because of violence or health reasons);

⇨ having a legal right to accommodation that you cannot access (e.g. if you have been illegally evicted);

⇨ living in accommodation you have no legal right to occupy (e.g. living in a squat or temporarily staying with friends).

Many people only associate homelessness with sleeping on the streets, but this conceals the range and scale of the problem. The reality is that the vast majority of homeless people are families or single people who are not 'sleeping rough'. Some may be staying with relatives and friends on a temporary basis. Others live in temporary accommodation, such as bed and breakfast hotels, hostels, night shelters and refuges. For many, this means living in poor quality accommodation that is detrimental to their health and well-being.

To understand what homelessness really is, it's important to first consider what a 'home' is. A home isn't just a roof over your head. It's a place that provides security, privacy, and links to a community and support network. It needs to be affordable, with support if necessary.

> *A home isn't just a roof over your head. It's a place that provides security, privacy, and links to a community and support network*

'Homelessness means loss, loss, loss... It is not just the loss of a home, maybe of a partner or of family life, of supportive friends or of a known community. It involves the loss of confidence and self-esteem. The loss of opportunities. These losses are less obvious... and the long-term effects on children in particular, and the stigma of homelessness, are not ever really taken on board. It's not just the reasons why people become homeless that are important but what it does to you.'
Health worker[1]

The original duties to homeless people were placed on local authorities by the Housing (Homeless Persons) Act 1977. The current duties are set out in the Housing Act 1996, which was amended by the Homelessness Act 2002, and place local authorities under a duty to rehouse certain homeless people. However, it is important to note that not everyone who falls under the above definition of homelessness will qualify for accommodation.

SHELTER

Households entitled to help with housing

There is an immediate duty on the local authority to provide interim accommodation for anyone they have reason to believe may be homeless and in priority need whilst they investigate the individual's circumstances.

Many people only associate homelessness with sleeping on the streets, but this conceals the range and scale of the problem

To access long-term housing under the homelessness legislation, a household must make an application to a local authority. The local authority has a duty to house individuals or households who meet the following criteria:

⇨ eligible for assistance – which will not apply to certain people who have lived abroad;

⇨ legally classed as homeless – by having nowhere that is available and reasonable to occupy, anywhere in the world;

⇨ in priority need – applying to all households that contain a pregnant woman or are responsible for dependent children; to some households made up of a 16- to 17-year-old or a care leaver aged 18 to 21; or where someone in the household is vulnerable, e.g. because of old age, mental or physical health problems; or by being in prison, care or the Armed Forces;

⇨ unintentionally homeless – those who have not deliberately done, or failed to do, something that caused them to become homeless, such as failing to make rent or mortgage payments when they could have afforded to do so.

Authorities also have a duty to continue to provide temporary accommodation for these households until

settled accommodation can be found for them. For further information on the local authority's duty to provide accommodation see the following page on Shelter's Get Advice channel: http://england.shelter.org.uk/get_advice/downloads_and_tools/emergency_checker

Households not entitled to help with housing

Many households who approach local authorities as homeless do not fit all four criteria above and therefore do not qualify for rehousing, even though they may have a serious housing need. For example, the local authority will not have a duty to house a family with children if they are deemed intentionally homeless. There will also be no duty owed to an asylum seeker as they will not be eligible due to their immigration status. Groups who do not qualify for assistance under the homelessness legislation may receive help from other agencies, for example social services departments or the UK Border Agency.

For a number of reasons many other people do not approach their local authority at all. A single person may feel he/she will not be regarded as a priority, others may have friends or family who have had a previous negative experience when seeking help. Many homeless people end up staying in hostels, or moving between friends and relatives. Some may sleep on the streets.

Notes

1 Collard, A. *Settling up towards a strategy for resettling homeless families*. London Housing Forum, London, 1997.

⇨ The above information is reprinted with kind permission from Shelter. Visit shelter.org.uk for more information.

Homelessness statistics

Legislation relating to homelessness differs somewhat between England, Scotland, Wales and Northern Ireland. Statistics are compiled separately for each country, rather than for the UK as a whole.

Legal definition of homelessness

In England the 1996 Housing Act states that a person or persons are defined as homeless if:

⇨ there is no accommodation that they are entitled to occupy;

⇨ they have accommodation but it is not reasonable for them to continue to occupy this accommodation;

⇨ they have accommodation but cannot secure entry to it;

⇨ they have accommodation but it consists of a moveable structure, vehicle or vessel designed or adapted for human habitation and there is no place where they are entitled or permitted both to place it and to reside in it.

Anyone meeting this definition and who has successfully applied to their local authority to be classified as such is officially recognised as being homeless.

Statutory homelessness

In England, people who are accepted by local authorities as being officially homeless, and who are deemed to have a priority need, are referred to as statutory homeless. Local authorities have a duty to accommodate people who are statutory homeless, as long as they also have a local connection and have not made themselves homeless intentionally.

The priority need groups include households with dependent children or a pregnant woman and people who are vulnerable in some way, for example because of mental illness or physical disability.

In 2002 an Order made under the 1996 Act extended the priority need categories to include: applicants aged 16 or 17; applicants aged 18 to 20 who were previously in care; applicants vulnerable as a result of time spent in care, in custody, or in HM Forces, and applicants vulnerable as a result of having to flee their home because of violence or the threat of violence.

Official homelessness figures

In England in 2007–08 local authorities made 130,840 decisions on applications for housing assistance under the homelessness legislation of the Housing Act 1996. Of these decisions, 63,170 resulted in the authority accepting the applicant as being statutory homeless. In addition, 31,360 applicants were deemed to be homeless, but either intentionally so or not in priority need.

As at 31st December 2008, 67,480 households in England were living in temporary accommodation.

The 2007–08 figures for England can be compared to the recent peak of 2003–04, when 135,430 households were accepted as statutory homeless and 80,650 were deemed to be intentionally homeless or not in priority need. The main reason for the peak at this particular time was the 2002 extension of the definition of priority need categories, as described above.

The number of households living in temporary accommodation reached its most recent high point in 2004, with 101,300 falling into this category.

(Source: Statutory Homelessness Statistical Releases, Department for Communities and Local Government)

In Scotland in 2007–08 there were 56,609 applications for housing assistance under Homeless Persons legislation. Of these, 32,111 were assessed as homeless and accorded priority status. In addition, 8,188 were assessed as homeless but not accorded priority status. There were 9,518 households living in temporary accommodation in Scotland as at 31st March 2008.

(Source: Operation of the Homeless Persons Legislation in Scotland, Scottish Executive)

OSW

In Wales there were 12,937 applications to local authorities under housing legislation in 2007–08. Of these applications, 6,367 were accepted as statutory homeless, and a further 2,864 were recognised as homeless but deemed to be intentionally so, or not in priority need. In September 2008 there were 2,952 households living in temporary accommodation.

(Source: National Statistics on Homelessness, Welsh Assembly Government)

In Northern Ireland in 2007–08 there were 19,030 applications to local authorities under homelessness legislation. From these, 9,234 were accepted as statutory homeless, and an additional 3,928 were categorised as homeless but intentionally so, or not in priority need.

(Source: Housing Statistics, Department for Social Development Northern Ireland)

As at 31st December 2008, 67,480 households in England were living in temporary accommodation

Based on the above quoted statistics, we can produce an aggregate United Kingdom figure for 2007–08, indicating that 110,882 households were accepted as statutory homeless, and a further 46,340 as homeless but not owed a statutory duty.

Hidden homelessness

In addition to those people recognised as statutory homeless there are also a large number of homeless single adults, or couples without dependant children, who meet the legal definition of homelessness but not the criteria for priority need. Although some of these people are included in the figures quoted above, in many cases they will not have even applied for official recognition, knowing that they do not meet the criteria of priority need. Statistics provided by the Government will therefore not include all people in the country who actually meet the definition of homelessness. As a result, this group is often referred to as hidden homeless.

People falling into the hidden homeless category include:

⇨ rough sleepers;

⇨ people living in bed & breakfast or other temporary accommodation because they have no other option;

⇨ people living in hostels, night shelters, or refuges;

⇨ people due for discharge from institutions (e.g. prison, hospital) who have no accommodation to go to;

⇨ people who are squatting because they have no other option;

⇨ people who are at risk of eviction;

⇨ people who are living in severe overcrowding;

⇨ people who are staying with friends or family because they have no other option, and who are living in overcrowded conditions or where the owner or renter of the accommodation is dissatisfied with the arrangement.

In 2003, Crisis estimated that there were around 400,000 people falling into the 'hidden homeless' category in the UK at any given time.

(Source: How many, how much? Single homelessness and the question of numbers and cost. A report for Crisis by Peter Kenway and Guy Palmer from the New Policy Institute)

Rough sleepers

Rough sleepers include those people sleeping, or bedded down, in the open air (such as on the streets, or in doorways, parks or bus shelters), and people in buildings or other places not designed for habitation (such as barns, sheds, car parks, cars, derelict boats, or stations). Rough sleeping is currently at its lowest recorded level. Figures published by the Department for Communities and Local Government (DCLG) in June 2008, based on street counts conducted between January and May 2008, indicate that there were 483 people sleeping rough in England on any given night. This reflects a 74% decrease since 1998, when the Government introduced their strategy to reduce rough sleeping.

⇨ The above information is reprinted with kind permission from OSW. Visit www.osw.org.uk for more information.

© OSW

Causes and effects of homelessness

The causes and effects of homelessness are widely discussed. Often these are interchangeable, for example unemployment could have caused someone to lose their home, but unemployment could also be the result of becoming homeless.

Figures from the Department of Communities and Local Government (DCLG), detailing priority homeless acceptances for the last quarter of 2008, reveal that primary reason for loss of last settled home broke down as follows:

⇨ **23%** Parents unable or unwilling to accommodate

⇨ **14%** Relatives/friends unable or unwilling to accommodate

⇨ **13%** Domestic violence by partner

⇨ **11%** End of shorthold tenancy

⇨ **7%** Mortgage or rent arrears

⇨ **6%** Non-violent relationship breakdown with partner

⇨ **6%** Other violence or harassment

⇨ **6%** Loss of other rented housing

⇨ **4%** Left institutions, Local Authority care or HM Forces

⇨ **3%** Left Home Office asylum support accommodation

⇨ **7%** Other reasons

Homeless people are a very disadvantaged and excluded group

These figures only reflect applicants accepted as statutory homeless, and not people classed as 'hidden homeless', whose reasons for loss of accommodation might be different.

In more general terms, the homeless population tend to have a higher incidence of the following than the population as a whole:

⇨ Physical and/or mental health problems

⇨ Substance misuse

⇨ Unemployment

⇨ Basic skills needs

⇨ Dyslexia and other learning difficulties

⇨ Experience of sexual or physical abuse

⇨ Have spent time in care

⇨ Have spent time in the armed forces

⇨ Experience of the criminal justice system

⇨ Relationship breakdown

⇨ Problems accessing welfare benefits

Homeless people are a very disadvantaged and excluded group and this is highlighted in a number of ways:

⇨ Difficulties in accessing social housing or private rented housing

⇨ High rents in hostels can cause difficulties in finding work

⇨ Temporary accommodation (such as hostels) are often difficult and insecure environments to live in, to establish routines or to plan ahead

⇨ Poor access to medical services

⇨ Difficulties in opening bank accounts and access to other mainstream services

⇨ Stigma and harassment

⇨ Discrimination

⇨ Poverty

Without support, this can affect homeless people in a number of ways:

⇨ Loss of self-esteem

⇨ Becoming institutionalised

⇨ Deterioration of mental and physical health

⇨ Increase in substance misuse

⇨ Loss of ability and will to care for oneself

⇨ Increased danger of abuse and violence

⇨ Increased chance of entering the criminal justice system

⇨ Development of behavioural problems

⇨ The above information is reprinted with kind permission from OSW. Visit www.osw.org.uk for more information.

© OSW

MSO

Transitions/leaving an institution

Time spent in an institution such as care or prison can increase the risk of someone becoming homeless and there are large numbers of care leavers and ex-offenders in the homeless population and lower numbers who have spent time in the Armed Forces.

Recent data from homelessness day centres and accommodation projects across England shows that, on average:[1]

⇨ 18% of clients were prison leavers;

⇨ 14% of clients were care leavers;

⇨ 6% of clients were ex-service personnel.

The experiences that people have in an institution such as care, prison or the Armed Forces can trigger homelessness once they leave those surroundings. Likewise, an inability to cope with the adult, outside or civilian world can also lead to homelessness.

About 34% of London's rough sleeper population have been in prison

Care leavers

The lack of stability associated with being in care can mean care leavers tend to have lower levels of educational participation and attainment and higher levels of mental health problems.[2] All of this can store up problems for the future, meaning those in care might not just face problems when they are leaving care but also in later life – care leavers might also tend to have unstable career patterns and higher than average levels of unemployment.[3]

Added to this, around two-thirds of young people in care have left by the age of 18, while the average age of leaving home for all young people is 22. This means that care leavers have to attempt the transition to independence at a much younger age than other people and so might lack independent living skills.

Prison leavers

About 34% of London's rough sleeper population have previously been in prison.[4]

⇨ Around a third of prisoners are not living in permanent accommodation prior to imprisonment.

⇨ Up to a third of prisoners lose their housing while they are in custody.

⇨ Around a third of prisoners about to leave prison said that they had nowhere to stay.[5]

When compared to the general population, prisoners are more likely to have had disturbed childhoods, problems at school, literacy problems, a family history of criminality, mental health problems, unemployment, drug and alcohol problems and a history of homelessness.[6]

Ex-service personnel

Crisis research[7] in the mid 1990s suggested that around a quarter of the homeless population had spent timed in the Armed Forces. Since then, there has been a concerted effort from Government and other organisations to tackle the problem. Now only around 6% of both rough sleepers and the wider single homeless people are ex-service personnel.[8]

There are generally four distinct 'life history trajectories' or pathways into homelessness for ex-service personnel. Amongst homeless ex-service personnel there are those with vulnerabilities from childhood or adolescence; those who developed problems whilst in the Armed Forces; those who struggled to adjust to civilian life after discharge and those who only faced problems after an unrelated traumatic experience after discharge.[9]

Notes

1   Homeless Link (2009) *Survey of Needs and Provision (SNAP)*

2   Randall, G. & Brown S. (1999) *Prevention is better than cure*

3   Randall, G. & Brown S. (1999) *Prevention is better than cure*

4   Broadway (2009) *Street to Home, Annual Report for London, 1st April 2008 to 31st March 2009*

5   Social Exclusion Unit (2002) *Reducing re-offending by ex-prisoners*

6   Social Exclusion Unit (2002) *Reducing re-offending by ex-prisoners*

7   Randall, G. & Brown, S. (1994) *Falling Out: A Research Study of Homeless Ex-Service People*

8   Homeless Link (2009) *Survey of Needs and Provision (SNAP)* and Centre for Housing Policy, University of York (June 2008) *The Experiences of Homeless Ex-Service Personnel in London*

9   Centre for Housing Policy, University of York (June 2008) *The Experiences of Homeless Ex-Service Personnel in London*

⇨ The above information is reprinted with kind permission from Crisis. Visit www.crisis.org.uk for more.

© Crisis

CRISIS

Sofa surfing

When you think about homelessness, you might picture somebody living on the streets, sleeping rough. That's not the only form of homelessness, however. 'Sofa surfing' is a form of homelessness that affects many homeless young people.

What is it?

People who sofa surf have usually just left home, for whatever reason, and are staying with friends in accommodation that isn't that secure.

They may find themselves sleeping on a sofa in a shared living room for one or two nights before moving on to stay with another friend.

They'll usually have nowhere to put their stuff and will only be able to sleep when the rest of the house isn't using the room they're staying in.

A recent report by homeless charity Crisis claimed that 72 per cent of homeless people had 'sofa surfed' at one time or another.

Calum's story

Calum, 16, left home after a row with his mum and soon found himself staying at a mate's house. He tells us what it was like. 'I had to sleep on a camp bed in the dining room of my friend Pete's house. All I had with me was a bag with a few clothes.

'Every day I had to get up early and put the bed away so that Pete's family could have their breakfast. Pete's mum was cool with it, but his dad wasn't and kept saying I was going to have to get out, or pay my way in some way.

'Most nights, I couldn't sleep for worrying about what I was going to do next.'

Carrie's story

'Me and my boyfriend James were kipping on a mate's floor for a while until we got ourselves sorted. He didn't want us around too much because we got under his feet so we ended up sleeping rough for a couple of nights.

People who sofa surf are staying with friends in accommodation that isn't that secure

'We didn't know that we could get help because nobody told us; we just thought we had to work it out by ourselves.

'Eventually, a friend's mum was really worried about us and told us to go to our local Connexions advice centre. We did and they put us in touch with the local council.

'Because we were 16, they got us somewhere to stay in a B&B and then after a while, they managed to get us a little flat. If you're homeless you need to get help as soon as you can.'

Getting help

While sleeping on a mate's sofa may be better than sleeping rough, you still need a more secure place to stay.

If you find yourself sofa surfing with no guaranteed place to stay, you should contact your local council. Most people have a right to advice and help with finding somewhere, and the council won't turn you away without looking into your situation first.

⇨ Information from need2know. Visit www.need2know.co.uk for more information.

© need2know

NEED2KNOW

Homelessness trends

Information from the Department for Communities and Local Government.

Homelessness 'acceptances'

Homelessness acceptances* peaked in 2003/2004, and since then are 71 per cent lower, with year on year reductions. The latest statutory homelessness statistics for the July to September 2009 period showed a 28 per cent reduction in acceptances compared with the same period last year.

These reductions are a result of homelessness strategies and prevention measures being put in place by every local authority in England.

In 2002 the strengthening of the homelessness legislation and the extension of the priority need groups are in part responsible for the sharp increase in homelessness acceptances between 2002 and 2003.

* Households accepted as being owed the main homelessness duty by local authorities under the homelessness legislation.

Temporary accommodation

The number of households living in temporary accommodation has been falling since the end of 2005, following a period when numbers had been static at around 101,000. The number of households living in temporary accommodation at 30 September 2009 was 56,920.

> **The number of households living in temporary accommodation has been falling since the end of 2005, following a period when numbers had been static at around 101,000**

A wide range of temporary accommodation is used by local authorities to discharge their homelessness duties, but the vast majority of households (89 per cent) (and 94 per cent of families with children) are in self-contained accommodation.

73 per cent of households were in private sector accommodation, 15 per cent were in accommodation owned by social landlords and eight per cent were in hostel accommodation and women's refuges. Only four per cent of all households in temporary accommodation were in bed and breakfast accommodation.

Families with children in Bed and Breakfast

In March 2002 the Government announced its target to end the use of Bed and Breakfast hotels to accommodate families with children except in an emergency and then for no longer than six weeks, by the end of March 2004.

This target was achieved and is being sustained. Since April 2004, when the Homelessness (Suitability of Accommodation) (England) Order 2003 came into force, local authorities can no longer discharge their duty to families with children accepted as homeless by placing them in Bed and Breakfast accommodation for longer than six weeks.

> **Homelessness acceptances peaked in 2003/2004, and since then are 71 per cent lower, with year on year reductions**

Rough sleeping

In 1998 the Prime Minister set a target to reduce the number of people sleeping rough by at least two-thirds by 2002. This target was met a year early and is being sustained – currently a 75 per cent reduction on the 1998 baseline level – with 464 rough sleepers on any given night in England.

Numbers in temporary accommodation – forward trajectory

The Government has a challenging target to halve the number of households in temporary accommodation to 50,500 by 2010. Information provided by local authorities in their temporary accommodation action plans and in response to a survey indicates that they are on track to achieve the 50 per cent reduction. During the period July–September, for the first time we have surpassed the projection and are now 441 households ahead of the TA trajectory.

⇨ The above information is reprinted with kind permission from the Department for Communities and Local Government. Visit www.communities.gov.uk for more information.

Happiness matters

Homeless people's views about breaking the link between homelessness and mental ill health – extract.

Mental health needs

The vast majority – 85% overall of interviewees and questionnaire respondents – had either a diagnosed mental health problem or had concerns about their mental health. Compare this with rates in the general population – one in six, or some 17%, at any one point in time.

The graphs below show the breakdown by diagnosis, compared with the general population rates. For all our respondents, rates of mental illness are much higher. And, while only nine per cent of our interviewees actually reported a formal diagnosis of personality disorder, we know from other studies that this is unlikely to reflect the true picture, as personality disorders are very frequently undiagnosed and unreported. A more realistic estimate could be as many as 70%.

Recommendations:

⇨ All frontline homelessness services need to be aware that their clients are likely to have a range of mental health problems.

⇨ All frontline staff in homelessness services need training in basic mental health awareness and a thorough understanding of what to do if they believe a client may be in need of referral for assessment and treatment.

Emotional wellbeing

Poor mental wellbeing can severely affect physical health and people's ability to manage day-to-day life, and can lead to more severe mental illness. It is also a measure of people's own sense of self-worth, self-efficacy, and belonging.

We asked interviewees how they would score themselves on a scale of one to five (1=lowest; 5=highest) against a description of 'wellbeing' adapted from the WHO definition:

'Someone with good mental health is enjoying life and can cope with the stress in their lives. They have a positive sense of feeling good and they believe in themselves. They feel valuable in their community.'

The average overall score for current mental well-being was 3.25. People in the shelters and hostels reported the lowest levels. But this average score dropped sharply to 1.4 when we asked how they had felt at their lowest point ever (see graph on page 10). More than one in ten (13%) of interviewees said they had felt suicidal at their worst. By no means all these people had a diagnosed mental health problem.

Interviewees also described very high levels of underlying mental distress:

⇨ 76% often felt depressed;

⇨ 71% often felt anxious;

⇨ 51% often felt panicky;

⇨ 51% often felt confused;

⇨ 49% often felt like they couldn't cope; and

⇨ 67% often felt like they couldn't be bothered to get out of bed.

Two-thirds directly linked being homeless with their mental state. They described a deep loss of self-worth, depression, hopelessness and despair:

'I feel like it's me against the world.'

'Makes you lose your self worth.'

'Being on the street and people looking at me makes me angry.'

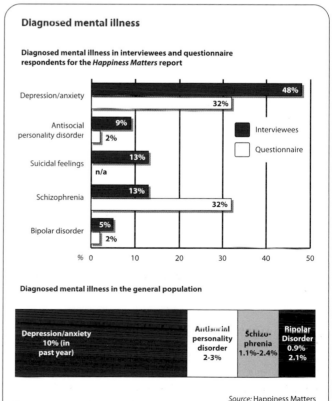

Diagnosed mental illness

Diagnosed mental illness in interviewees and questionnaire respondents for the *Happiness Matters* report

	Interviewees	Questionnaire
Depression/anxiety	48%	32%
Antisocial personality disorder	9%	2%
Suicidal feelings	13%	n/a
Schizophrenia	13%	32%
Bipolar disorder	5%	2%

Diagnosed mental illness in the general population

Depression/anxiety 10% (in past year)	Antisocial personality disorder 2-3%	Schizophrenia 1.1%-2.4%	Bipolar Disorder 0.9% 2.1%

Source: Happiness Matters report, St Mungo's, July 2009

ST MUNGO'S

'I feel like a low life and your friends tend to treat you differently.'

'Depression, boredom, dreams fade, lack of ambition.'

'Feel I want to die and it will solve the problem.'

'Makes you think about or turn to drugs.'

Nearly three-quarters said their mental health seriously affected their day-to-day life:

> **When asked what helps when you're feeling low, a significant number (38%) of our interviewees said they used alcohol or drugs. For more than two-thirds, this was directly related to their circumstances and poor mental health**

'It affects every aspect of my daily life... I do need support with structuring my time, coping with daily living and stress and support with my emotional state.'

'Makes every day normal tasks extremely hard picking up my giro, going to the doctors, paying rent, washing clothes.'

'Feel low in mood most days and feel unable to achieve anything with regards to my problems.'

'Affects my routine – on a bad day can't do anything or get anything done.'

Recommendation:

⇨ All services involved with homeless people need to be aware that, even if their clients do not have a formal diagnosis of mental ill health, they are likely to be experiencing poor emotional wellbeing that affects their chances of making a better life.

Drink and drugs

When asked what helps when you're feeling low, a significant number (38%) of our interviewees said they used alcohol or drugs. For more than two-thirds, this was directly related to their circumstances and poor mental health: 65% said they drank or took drugs 'because it is easier than coping with my life', including 67% of those who had a diagnosed mental health problem.

'Drinking! As it blocks it out.'

'Reading, music, smoking, a joint.'

'Go and buy some drugs.'

'Beer, spliff and some gear.'

'Drink and drugs, blocks out the depression.'

'When things are OK [with my mental health], fine but when things go wrong I drink and take more drugs to hide the problem.'

Mental health needs combined with substance misuse issues ('dual diagnosis') are extremely common among the homeless population – we know from our annual Client Needs Survey (2008) that more than half of St Mungo's clients are likely to have mental health and substance use needs.

> **Mental health needs combined with substance misuse issues ('dual diagnosis') are extremely common among the homeless population**

Even if homeless people do not have a formal dual diagnosis (and many do not meet the threshold), the mental health or substance use may be impeding their progress towards a more settled life. Experience from St Mungo's dual diagnosis projects provides ample evidence that substance and mental health needs should be addressed together.

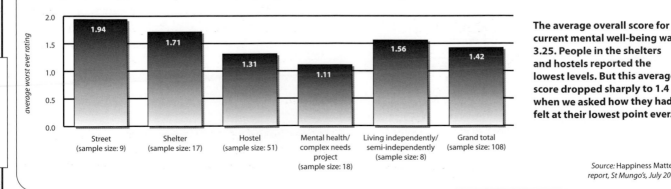

Average self-ratings of worst ever mental well-being (scale = 1- 5 where 5 is highest)

The average overall score for current mental well-being was 3.25. People in the shelters and hostels reported the lowest levels. But this average score dropped sharply to 1.4 when we asked how they had felt at their lowest point ever.

Source: Happiness Matters report, St Mungo's, July 2009

ST MUNGO'S

Recommendations:

⇨ Services need to stop approaching drink, drugs and mental health as separate issues. For the vast majority of homeless people they are a part of the individual's range of needs and must be addressed as a whole. Drink and drugs are often used to deal with difficulties in homeless people's lives – we need to tackle the addiction and the life.

⇨ A typical homeless client, who has experience of, or is vulnerable to, sleeping rough, will likely have highly complex needs involving poor emotional wellbeing, possible mental illness, likely personality disorder and poly-substance use. 'All-in-one' approaches are the only way to deal with these issues.

Respondents were asked 'To what extent do you agree or disagree with the following statement? The Government should be doing more to help prevent those who are at risk from losing their home'. % strongly agree/tend to agree.

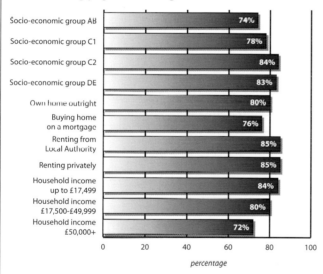

Socio-economic group AB	74%
Socio-economic group C1	78%
Socio-economic group C2	84%
Socio-economic group DE	83%
Own home outright	80%
Buying home on a mortgage	76%
Renting from Local Authority	85%
Renting privately	85%
Household income up to £17,499	84%
Household income £17,500-£49,999	80%
Household income £50,000+	72%

percentage

Respondents were asked 'If you were to find yourself in the position of being homeless, which people or organisations, if any, do you think you would turn to to provide you with accommodation?'. Mentions of 1% or higher.

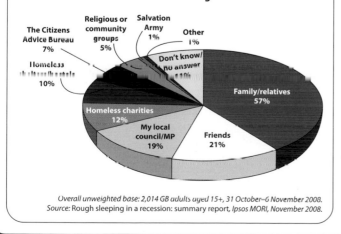

- The Citizens Advice Bureau 7%
- Religious or community groups 5%
- Salvation Army 1%
- Other 1%
- Don't know/no answer 1%
- Homeless charities [hostels] 10%
- Family/relatives 57%
- Homeless charities 12%
- My local council/MP 19%
- Friends 21%

Overall unweighted base: 2,014 GB adults aged 15+, 31 October–6 November 2008.
Source: Rough sleeping in a recession: summary report, Ipsos MORI, November 2008.

Rough sleepers

Rough sleepers are the hardest group to reach in surveys like this. In addition to the nine rough sleepers and 17 people using our emergency shelters, who were very recently off the streets, we talked to five outreach workers.

The rough sleepers gave the impression that their mental wellbeing was fine – better than any of the other groups in the survey. But the outreach workers told us a very different story. In their view, a minimum of 60%, and maybe even 100% of their clients probably had a serious mental health problem and the vast majority used drugs or alcohol.

'Some are mentally ok but still finding it stressful/difficult/depressing/isolating which in turn makes it harder to cope and deal with day to day things like appointments/staff other people/procedures and the longer it goes on the more likely they are to develop further problems mental/physical or substance use.'

'I felt so low and degraded living on the streets and taking drugs'

Clearly rough sleepers are a particularly vulnerable sub-group of homeless people, with high levels of mental health needs. This is how some of the rough sleepers described their daily lives:

'Every day is a challenge'

'Makes you think about or turn to drugs'

'I felt so low and degraded living on the streets and taking drugs'

'I don't look forward to night time as during the day you can always find something to do i.e. libraries, parks, indoor shopping centre etc'

Recommendation:

⇨ People sleeping rough on the streets have mental health and substance use needs over and above those of the general homeless population. Urgent action and effective, prolonged engagement is needed to target people whose mental ill health is keeping them on the streets.

July 2009

⇨ The above information is an extract from the executive summary of St Mungo's *Happiness Matters* report and is reprinted with permission. Visit www.mungos.org for more.

© St Mungo's

Homelessness – it makes you sick

Information from St Mungo's.

The problem

It is perhaps well known that homeless people are not healthy. However, we continue to be shocked by the levels of ill health our residents endure. In our hostels last year, we found that: 32% of our residents had an alcohol dependency; 63% had a drugs problem; 49% had a mental health problem; and 43% had a physical illness. The great majority of rough sleepers – over two-thirds – have multiple needs, often a combination of a mental health problem with (poly) substance misuse, usually involving multiple physical health problems, and sometimes accompanied by a non-compliant attitude falling into the 'challenging behaviour' category.

Our recent research highlights the real health problems of homeless people and the struggles they face in accessing basic healthcare.

Health and homeless

Homelessness exacerbates existing conditions, and may give rise to new ones. The most common illnesses to affect residents in our hostels include:

⇨ Circulatory disease;

⇨ Cardio-vascular problems;

⇨ Epilepsy and neurological problems;

⇨ Gastro-intestinal disorders;

⇨ Liver disease;

⇨ Inflammation of the joints;

⇨ Pulmonary disease.

We have also identified clients suffering from TB, renal failure, abscesses, deep vein thrombosis, and blood-borne viruses, especially Hepatitis C. Perhaps the most telling detail is that, in the middle of London in the 21st century, we are seeing cases of trenchfoot. Over half of interviewees in our research had a long-term condition.

Healthcare services failing the homeless

Despite these illnesses, one in three interviewees had a condition for which they were not being treated; and over half of this group was estimated to have conditions which could deteriorate to the point where they would require urgent medical attention. It is not then surprising that ambulances were called to St Mungo's on average twice a week.

More tellingly, 85% of all ambulance calls were for illness or overdose, and our data show that most call-outs were for pre-existing conditions (asthma; diabetes; heart and circulation problems; epilepsy; respiratory difficulties; stomach or liver complaints; substance use crises) which had reached emergency status. Although we cannot quantify it precisely, it is undoubtedly the case that enhanced primary care could have prevented some of this usage of crisis services.

Our research showed that:

⇨ At least two-thirds of call-outs result in a trip to hospital, of which the majority (67%) are visits to A&E. 42% of all ambulance call-outs end up in A&E. 24% result in hospitalisation.

⇨ Only a very small number overall (17%) came away with a treatment plan. Even after hospitalisation only 30% come away with a treatment plan.

⇨ 49% of interviewed clients have experienced a negative contact with A&E or hospital.

⇨ A third of interviewees (33%) reported experiencing difficulties accessing health services.

⇨ 18% of clients don't use a GP at all and 41% use a GP 'as necessary', which, given the high incidence of medical conditions, could indicate they are not making good decisions about their own healthcare (i.e. most of them probably ought to be attending regularly).

- One in three interviewees has a condition for which they are not receiving treatment at all.

- The death rate in St Mungo's hostels is one per month and clients are, on average, only 41 when they die and 50% are under 40 when they die.

Clients interviewed as part of our research were quick to suggest potential solutions to the inequalities experienced by homeless people within the health service. These included:

- 47% of interviewees, when asked to suggest ideas, said the most important medical services a project should have are general primary health services (Doctor/Nurse).

- 75% of interviewees rated as 'High' importance the proposal that a full package of primary healthcare provisions be provided in every project.

- Health Support Workers and Hospital Discharge Workers were also considered to be highly important by a significant majority of clients (64% and 56%, respectively). These workers provide a link between homeless people and NHS services and ensure that homeless people always leave hospital with a treatment plan in place if one is needed.

September 2008

Homelessness exacerbates existing conditions, and may give rise to new ones

- The above information is an extract from St Mungo's summary report *Homelessness: it makes you sick*, and is reprinted with permission. Visit www.mungos.org/campaigns/homelessness_it_makes_you_sick

Drunk and overdosing homeless people put strain on NHS

One drink- or drug-addicted homeless person is admitted to hospital every three hours, putting a severe strain on the National Health Service, new figures show.

By Rosa Prince, Political Correspondent

The rate of drug and drink-related admissions of homeless people has risen by 117 per cent since 2004, with six out of ten hospital trusts reporting that numbers have gone up in the last five years.

Many of the rough sleepers had overdosed or suffered infections from using dirty needles to inject drugs such as heroin, while others needed their stomachs pumped after drinking too much.

The figures, contained in a series of answers to freedom of information requests put in to 173 hospital trusts, were released by the Conservatives, who issued a report setting out the importance of understanding the health needs of homeless people.

In particular, the party wants the availability of cheap alcohol in supermarkets to be curtailed, and for health boards to work with local homeless charities such as Shelter to consider the best ways to help homeless people in their area.

Grant Shapps, the shadow housing minister, said: 'A refusal to confront the extent of the homlessness issue in the United Kingdom leaves our frontline services such as the NHS struggling to cope.

'Our report demonstrates how drugs and alcohol frequently play a major role in perpetuating the chaotic lives lived by many people trapped in homelessness.

'This is one of the reasons why Conservatives will fix the crazy situation whereby supermarkets are selling high strength lager for less than they charge for a bottle of water.'

The report shows that nearly 14,000 homeless people were admitted to hospital with drink and drug-related conditions in the last five years, the equivalent of eight a day or one rough sleeper every three hours.

London had the most admissions, followed by Liverpool and Leeds.

More than ten per cent of rough sleepers who ended up in hospital for alcohol or drugs were under the age of 25, even though young people are estimated to account for between six and seven per cent of the homeless population.

A spokesman for the Department of Health said: 'We know that around 50 per cent of rough sleepers have a problem with alcohol – for some this is linked to mental health issues and other addictions.

'The Government is taking action to end rough sleeping once and for all.'

1 January 2010

ST MUNGO'S / THE TELEGRAPH

Asylum seeker suffering hits new depths as destitution lasts for years

One in three now homeless for over a year, says report.

A major report today exposes the worsening crisis amongst refused asylum seekers in the UK, as it reveals that more than a third have now been destitute for over a year, with two out of every three of those homeless originating from some of the most troubled countries in the world.

The independent report commissioned by the Joseph Rowntree Charitable Trust (JRCT) warns that suffering amongst the destitute is reaching new depths and today calls for an immediate temporary amnesty for 'unreturnable' asylum seekers.

The report, *Still Destitute*, shows that:

⇨ More than a third of all refused asylum seekers – including children – have been homeless for a year or more. Community health teams say many are now suffering mental illness and malnutrition because of their prolonged destitution.

⇨ Destitution is linked to country of origin, with two out of every three homeless asylum seekers coming from just four countries: Iraq, Iran, Eritrea and Zimbabwe – countries where it is difficult or impossible to arrange safe route of return because of ongoing conflict, violence or human rights abuses.

⇨ The Government's own figures show that a fifth of legacy cases can't currently be returned because of factors beyond its control.

Joseph Rowntree Charitable Trust trustee Peter Coltman said: 'We must no longer ignore the shameful suffering of people, many of whom – the evidence clearly shows – simply can't go home.

'That is why today we urge the Government to grant temporary leave to all those who, through no fault of their own, cannot return to their country of origin. It is also why we implore the Government to implement the rational and reasonable recommendations that the JRCT commission made three years ago and end the shame of asylum seeker destitution.'

Still Destitute is based on a survey conducted in Leeds, one of the principal UK dispersal centres, and is the third in a series of annual reports designed by JRCT to provide comparable snapshots of asylum seeker destitution in the UK.

Still Destitute also shows:

⇨ Voluntary, charity and faith-based agencies set up to support homeless asylum seekers are close to financial breaking point and suffering increasing incidents of aggression from desperate asylum seekers.

⇨ Destitution is not simply an issue for 'legacy cases' – the amount of destitution resulting from the Government's New Asylum Model has increased by a third since last year (from 45 to 60 individuals).

⇨ One in every three refused asylum seekers is destitute because of administrative delays in processing (though destitution as a result of bureaucratic error among those still applying has fallen).

The report urges the Government to grant temporary leave to remain for people who cannot return to their country of origin through no fault of their own; abolish section 4 support and make continuation of support automatic on refusal of asylum until the individual leaves the UK; recognise validity of religious, social and family connections for refugees in need of housing.

The JRCT repeats previously unheeded calls for the Government to:

⇨ End the destitution of asylum seekers and refugees at all stages of the asylum process.

⇨ Create systems to ensure no child or their parents are left destitute.

⇨ Give asylum seekers at all stages a license to work so they can contribute to the UK and provide for themselves.

⇨ Ensure asylum seekers at all stages of the process are eligible for and can access primary and secondary health care and have access to proper legal representation.

Notes

⇨ The 2008 and 2009 reports both show that Zimbabwe (which currently has no diplomatic relationship with the UK) is the single biggest country of origin for refused asylum seekers. While the total number of refused asylum seekers recorded was down from last year's 266 to this year's 232, a combination of factors suggest the real current figure could be a lot higher.

⇨ National Audit Office figures for 2009 show that a fifth of 'legacy' cases cannot currently be resolved (be removed or given leave to stay here) because of what the UK Borders Agency refers to as 'external factors'.

⇨ Legacy cases are cases dealt with before the 2007 introduction of the New Asylum Model. The Model (NAM) was introduced to speed up decisions on asylum applications and manage cases through to conclusion of integration for refugees or removal of refused asylum seekers.

⇨ 'Section 4' support is available to refused asylum seekers who have no other means of support and who are 'taking all reasonable steps' to leave the UK. It may also be granted if there is a physical or medical reason why they cannot travel or because they are seeking a judicial review.

⇨ The lack of diplomatic relationship with a country (as in the case of the UK/Zimbabwe – the single most common country of origin for refused asylum seekers) makes formal return of a refused asylum seeker impossible.

9 July 2009

⇨ The above information is reprinted with kind permission from the Joseph Rowntree Charitable Trust. Visit www.jrct.org.uk for more information.

© Joseph Rowntree Charitable Trust

Destitution: asylum's untold story

One afternoon in August 2003, Esrafil, a 29-year-old asylum seeker from Iran, attended Refugee Action's Asylum Advice office in Manchester city centre. He went to the toilets, doused himself in a flammable liquid, returned to the front desk and, without warning, set himself alight with a lighter. Esrafil was taken to hospital with severe burns. Six days later, he died of his injuries.

At the time of his shocking and tragic death, Esrafil had been left destitute after his asylum application was refused. Many avenues of assistance are being closed off to asylum seekers, who are facing hunger, humiliation and helplessness. For frightened and desperate clients with very limited options, ours is often the only door that remains open to them.

Many rejected asylum seekers are unable to return to their countries of origin through no fault of their own. Those from countries such as Somalia cannot be returned because there are few, if any, viable and safe routes available. Other countries of origin are unwilling to accept asylum seekers back if they do not have the necessary travel documents.

Under Section 4 of the 2002 Nationality, Immigration and Asylum Act, failed asylum seekers have had state support withdrawn unless they agree to sign up to return home voluntarily. This applies even to those who cannot be returned because it is unsafe. As a result many asylum seekers, who are often terrified at the prospect of returning home, are being left in a kind of limbo, banned from working yet unable to access benefits.

Harsh new Government legislation threatens to further marginalise asylum seekers. Failed asylum seeking families – until now supported under the Children Act – will face destitution if they do not agree to return home. If they fail to co-operate, their children could be taken into care. Even failed asylum seekers who agree to return voluntarily will soon be forced to undertake community work in order to receive accommodation and food.

The Government has also made it a criminal offence – punishable by up to two years in prison – to arrive in the UK without valid travel documents, despite the fact that many asylum seekers are pressured into destroying their documents by agents.

New restrictions on legal aid have also made it much more difficult for asylum seekers fleeing persecution to get a full and fair hearing of their case. Restrictions on access to healthcare for failed asylum seekers will mean that many destitute people suffering acute ill health are denied treatment.

In a recent Refugee Action survey, almost one in three of our clients said they had experienced homelessness and 57 per cent had had a period when they had no money to live on. 40 per cent said they had a health problem.

⇨ The above information is reprinted courtesy of Refugee Action: visit www.refugee-action.org.uk for more information.

© Refugee Action

Rough sleeping

Key facts.

Introduction

Homeless Link supports the new rough sleeping strategy. We are committed to turning the vision of ending rough sleeping into a reality.

Since the Social Exclusion Unit report on rough sleeping was published in 1998 there has been substantial progress towards the aim of ending rough sleeping.

So far...

⇨ The total number of people found rough sleeping by local authority street counts has fallen by nearly three-quarters – from 1,850 in 1998 to 464 in 2009.[1]

⇨ Over 9,000 people have been helped off the streets of London since 2000,[2] so while there remains a constant flow of people onto the streets, most people do not remain on the streets for the long term.

The total number of people found rough sleeping by local authority street counts has fallen by nearly three-quarters – from 1,850 in 1998 to 464 in 2009

Rough sleeping is the most visible form of homelessness, but despite this, there is limited data available. We have set out below some key statistics.

1. How many are sleeping rough?

In the 1990s, the voluntary sector and the Government agreed the 'street count'[3] – a consistent way to measure rough sleeping. This method reveals the absolute minimum level of rough sleeping rather than the full extent.

England

⇨ Last year, 76 street counts were carried out. They found a total of 464 people sleeping rough in England on any given night, a reduction from the previous year's figure of 483.

London

⇨ The total of local authority street counts in London last year was 265 (57% of the total for the whole of England).

⇨ The counts found the highest number of rough sleepers in the London boroughs of Westminster (110), City of London (38) and Tower Hamlets (17).

⇨ Figures from a London-based recording system[4] show that 3,472 people were seen rough sleeping in the capital last year. This is 455 more than last year.

⇨ Over 9,000 people have been helped off the streets of London since 2000.[5]

2. Profile

Profiles of people sleeping rough differ in different parts of the country. Information in this section refers to London, for which the most comprehensive data is available[6].

Gender

⇨ 87% of people contacted were male and 13% were female.

Age

⇨ 61% were aged between 26 and 45. 31% were aged over 46 and 8% were under age 25.

Ethnicity/nationality

⇨ 49% were 'white British' and 13% were 'black or black British'. 19% were 'white other', 7% were 'white Irish' and 3% were 'Asian' or 'Asian British'.

⇨ 62% were of UK nationality, and a further 14% were nationals of recent EU accession states.[7]

Support needs

⇨ Of those whose support needs are known, 40% had drug problems, 49% had alcohol problems and 35% had mental health problems. (People may be counted in more than one category.) 17% had neither drug, alcohol or mental health problems. These proportions have remained consistent over the last five years.

3. Where have rough sleepers come from and where do they go to?

⇨ Approximately 39% have been in prison, 12% in care and 5% in the Armed Forces at some time in their lives. (Some people may have experience of more than one of these.)

⇨ There is a constant flow of people onto the streets, but most people are not on the streets for the long term. Last year, 58% were new to the streets. 26% were also seen rough sleeping in the year before, and 16% were first seen rough sleeping more than five years ago.[8]

⇨ Last year, of the rough sleepers that were seen, 35% were either reconnected or booked into accommodation.

4. Facilities for rough sleepers[9]

⇨ Nationally, there are 183 day centres serving an estimated 10,000 people per day.

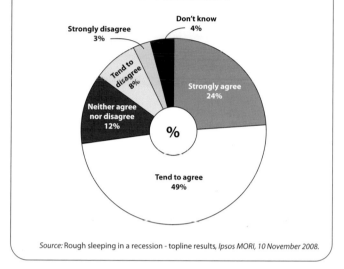

Respondents were asked 'To what extent do you agree or disagree with the following statement? "The number of people sleeping rough or living on the street is likely to increase because of the current economic situation"'.

Don't know 4%
Strongly disagree 3%
Tend to disagree 8%
Strongly agree 24%
Neither agree nor disagree 12%
%
Tend to agree 49%

Source: Rough sleeping in a recession - topline results, Ipsos MORI, 10 November 2008.

⇨ There are an estimated 50,000 bed spaces in direct access hostels and second stage accommodation for non-statutory homeless people in England.

⇨ There are 263 direct access hostels in England, and at least 1,084 second stage accommodation projects.

Notes

1 Data from Communities and Local Government.

2 CHAIN (Combined Homeless Action and Information Network) (2009).

3 http://www.communities.gov.uk/housing/homelessness/roughsleeping/

4 CHAIN (Combined Homeless Action and Information Network) (2009) 'Street to Home' Annual Report for London 1st April 2008 to 31st March 2009.

5 CHAIN (Combined Homeless Action and Information Network) (2009) 'Street to Home' Annual Report for London 1st April 2008 to 31st March 2009.

6 CHAIN (Combined Homeless Action and Information Network) (2009) 'Street to Home' Annual Report for London 1st April 2008 to 31st March 2009.

7 These are the 'A8' (Czech Republic, Estonia, Latvia, Lithuania, Hungary, Poland, Slovakia and Slovenia) and Romania and Bulgaria (the 'A2').

8 These people have not necessarily been rough sleeping continuously since they were first seen.

9 Homeless Link (2009) Survey of Needs and Provision.

⇨ The above information is reprinted with kind permission from Homeless Link. Visit www.homeless.org.uk for more information.

© Homeless Link

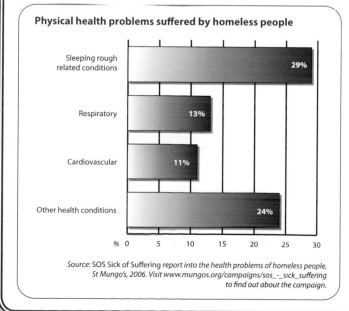

Physical health problems suffered by homeless people

Sleeping rough related conditions — 29%
Respiratory — 13%
Cardiovascular — 11%
Other health conditions — 24%

% 0 5 10 15 20 25 30

Source: SOS Sick of Suffering report into the health problems of homeless people, St Mungo's, 2006. Visit www.mungos.org/campaigns/sos_-_sick_suffering to find out about the campaign.

Life on the streets

Information from The Scotsman.

By Martyn McLaughlin

Gary does not know how much money he makes. His hourly rate varies. Sometimes it's no more than a clenched palm of silver. Often, a pound coin will glimmer in the lining of the jacket he lays before him and, on occasion, a note too.

The amount is dependent on a host of circumstances: his mood, the time of day, the weather, even last night's football results. 'With the state the football in Scotland's in, that's no' good news for me,' he jokes.

A thin, friendly man in his early thirties, Gary has been begging on the streets of Glasgow for the past seven months. His descent to the streets began when he was paid off from his job in a warehouse, and was evicted from his private let after failing to keep up with rent.

No-one knows for sure how many people like Gary there are on the nation's streets, but estimates suggest their numbers are only a few hundred strong

He is a recovering heroin addict, but has been clean for nearly two years. He says drugs are commonplace among those who beg on the streets, but that he tries not to associate with them.

In the half-hour I spend talking to him in the Cowcaddens area, two people give him a total of 60 pence. At night, he sleeps in a nearby hostel. He aims to make around £10 a day to cover his food – although one office worker buys him lunch from Greggs most days – with the rest going towards a deposit for a flat. Sometimes, he admits, he will spend money on alcohol.

'I'm trying to get myself sorted, but it's hard keeping positive,' he explains. 'I'm not here to get enough for a bag or make a wage. I just want enough to get on my feet.'

No-one knows for sure how many people like Gary there are on the nation's streets, but estimates suggest their numbers are only a few hundred strong. As one of the most potent symbols of social exclusion in 21st-century Scotland, one would expect a bulging dossier of studies relating to begging, material with which to offer guidance as to how best to eradicate a shaming problem. Yet there is a paucity of research, the majority of which involves small-scale studies of a few dozen people, and dates back to the 1990s.

Information on the begging population in urban areas is not gathered by local authorities, nor by homelessness charities. As one academic told The Scotsman, begging is considered an 'awkward' field of research.

However, the void where statistics should be is filled by anecdotal claims that the problem is getting worse. That was the position this week of Ivan Artolli, general manager of the Balmoral, one of Edinburgh's most prestigious hotels. 'You do not have the same problem in London, Paris, Brussels, Florence or Frankfurt,' Mr Artolli told The Scotsman. 'I have been writing to anyone I know in the city, because I think this is quite unacceptable. I have worked in 15 places across Europe and I have never come across a city with such tolerance of beggars.'

Mr Artolli is not alone in his view that such a tolerance is on the wane across the capital. The begging issue was high on the agenda at a recent meeting of Morningside Community Council, whose members are keen to see the introduction of a by-law in the city which would ban beggars outright from taking up their pitches. Such policies have been mooted before, but as legislation stands, begging is not an offence. Only when its perpetrators resort to aggressive tactics can they be prosecuted under breach of the peace laws or antisocial behaviour orders.

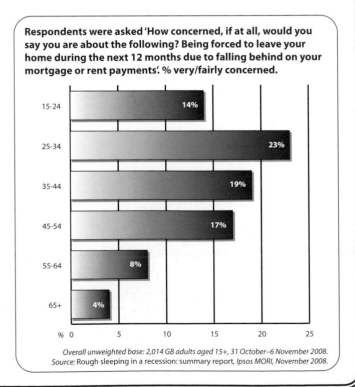

Respondents were asked 'How concerned, if at all, would you say you are about the following? Being forced to leave your home during the next 12 months due to falling behind on your mortgage or rent payments'. % very/fairly concerned.

Age	%
15-24	14%
25-34	23%
35-44	19%
45-54	17%
55-64	8%
65+	4%

Overall unweighted base: 2,014 GB adults aged 15+, 31 October–6 November 2008.
Source: Rough sleeping in a recession: summary report, Ipsos MORI, November 2008.

Quite how many beggars there are on Edinburgh's streets is unclear. The most recent statistics from the Scottish Government show there were 685 households living in temporary accommodation in March 2009, with 4,704 homeless households last year. Of those who applied for homelessness assistance, some ten per cent reported sleeping rough the night before. But taken together, these figures cannot establish how many people beg – not all who do so are homeless, for example, while not every rough sleeper begs.

As Dr Ian McIntosh, a senior lecturer and head of applied social science at the University of Stirling, and one of the few academics to research begging, points out: 'The actual statistics for the numbers of people begging are very difficult to work out. It's looked at as an awkward subject. People have always said there's a rise in the number of beggars on the streets, but we don't know.'

While the numbers are unclear, researchers and charities warn that overwhelmingly, those who beg do so out of desperate circumstances. A Joseph Rowntree Foundation report, which surveyed scores of people begging, sleeping rough, or selling the *Big Issue* in Edinburgh and Glasgow, found that begging is a 'survival strategy overwhelmingly driven by need not greed'.

Most of those interviewed told of a family background blighted by trauma and mental health issues, while almost half had been in residential school or foster care. Others reported growing up with parents who were drug users, while those involved in substance abuse took it up at an early age in an attempt to cope with painful experiences.

According to Crisis, the national charity for single homeless people, there is little financial gain to be made out of begging. While some London councils have reported that beggars can earn up to £300 a day, Crisis says the average individual is fortunate to find £10 to £20 left in their hat or cup. As Orwell once said, it is a trade 'at which it is impossible to grow rich'.

'The UK is the fifth richest country in the world and yet there are still people who feel they have no choice but to take to the streets to beg,' said Graeme Brown, director of the housing and homelessness charity, Shelter Scotland. 'Shelter does not condone aggressive begging in the slightest. It is unacceptable and should not be tolerated. However, most people do not beg because it's an easy option – some feel they have no choice. For many they may beg because they are unable to access help.'

A Joseph Rowntree Foundation report, which surveyed scores of people begging, sleeping rough, or selling the Big Issue in Edinburgh and Glasgow, found that begging is a 'survival strategy overwhelmingly driven by need not greed'

Yet what compassion exists amongst the public for the grim life on those forced out on to the streets is often undone by those 'professional' beggars. There has been increasing resentment towards the numbers of eastern European migrants often working as part of gangs across the country's cities, the vast majority of whom are not homeless. The *Big Issue*, the magazine set up to help homeless people find their feet, has even banned some of its Romanian vendors for aggressive selling in Glasgow.

Of those migrants who beg, some play musical instruments, others are surrounded by their children,

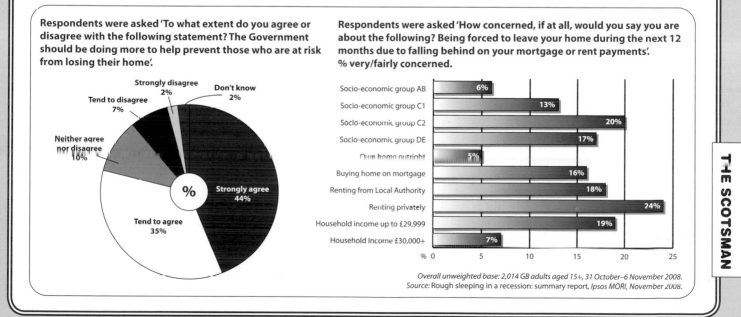

Respondents were asked 'To what extent do you agree or disagree with the following statement? The Government should be doing more to help prevent those who are at risk from losing their home'.

- Strongly disagree 2%
- Don't know 2%
- Tend to disagree 7%
- Neither agree nor disagree 10%
- Strongly agree 44%
- Tend to agree 35%

Respondents were asked 'How concerned, if at all, would you say you are about the following? Being forced to leave your home during the next 12 months due to falling behind on your mortgage or rent payments'. % very/fairly concerned.

- Socio-economic group AB: 6%
- Socio-economic group C1: 13%
- Socio-economic group C2: 20%
- Socio-economic group DE: 17%
- Own home outright: 5%
- Buying home on mortgage: 16%
- Renting from Local Authority: 18%
- Renting privately: 24%
- Household income up to £29,999: 19%
- Household income £30,000+: 7%

Overall unweighted base: 2,014 GB adults aged 15+, 31 October–6 November 2008.
Source: Rough sleeping in a recession: summary report, Ipsos MORI, November 2008.

THE SCOTSMAN

while the tactic of offering fake gold has been noted, too. Only two months ago, a group of eastern European men were spotted on several occasions standing at the side of the M9 next to a battered M-registration Mercedes, trying to flag down traffic. Those motorists who stopped were not asked for a jump-start, but money.

According to Crisis, the national charity for single homeless people, there is little financial gain to be made out of begging

But on the south side of Glasgow, one Latvian woman told *The Scotsman* that she deplored such ruses. Emilija said she has been in Scotland for just over a year, and worked in a restaurant until November. 'I was told I have not enough National Insurance contributions, so I have no money,' she said. 'I live with my sister but until we find a job I have to do this.' The 25-year-old said she is regularly subject to abuse. 'I am not Roma, but people think I am. I have been shouted at and spat on, but all I want is enough money to live with.'

Such mistrust is not a surprise to Dr McIntosh. In his study, which looked at how people perceive beggars on Edinburgh's Princes Street, he found that shopworkers

attempted to pinpoint those 'legitimate' beggars before handing over money, often seeking out quasi-romantic notions of the vagrant.

'I feel sorry for the old guys,' one man in his fifties said. 'They've been on the road for years, that weatherbeaten look they've got, just their appearance on their face, maybe you can get make-up, I don't know, but they just look genuine.'

Others, however, proved more cynical. 'You've got other ones that probably have a £100,000 house somewhere, jump into their car and, you know, it's easy money for them,' said one respondent.

'People tend to have an ambivalent attitude towards begging,' Dr McIntosh said. 'They jockey between feelings of sympathy, then being harsh about it. If you dropped 50 pence running for a bus, you probably would keep running and not be bothered about it. But giving the same amount of money to a beggar has a moral aspect. People feel some embarrassment and guilt about whose fault it is.'

War of words over need for new laws

Aberdeen was the first city in Scotland to try to introduce a by-law that would ban begging outright. First mooted six years ago, the campaign stemmed from research that found a general begging population in Scotland's oil capital around 25 strong. Some of those individuals, the council said, were not homeless.

A year later, Edinburgh City Council echoed the calls, while Scotland's biggest local authority in Glasgow stated the case for additional powers in the consultation for the Civic Government Scotland Act. The attempt to put the measure in place failed, however, with the previous administration ruling that there was no need for new legislation. Since then, the matter has refused to go away. Bill Aitken, the Tory MSP, has raised the possibility of a member's bill to crack down on aggressive begging.

Justice secretary Kenny MacAskill has said he believes there is no need for a by-law, with police able to deal with aggressive begging through existing laws covering breach of the peace and antisocial behaviour orders.

In the first scheme of its kind in Scotland, Aberdeen City Council introduced begging boxes in an attempt to curb aggressive begging, but after just three months, the five outlets raised a total of just £348, and were relocated to shopping centres after being repeatedly targeted by thieves.

27 January 2010

THE SCOTSMAN

Young people and homelessness

Every year, thousands of young people leave home before they reach 18. While some are able to find suitable housing, many others become homeless. With the absence of a stable living environment, young people often find it difficult to continue in education or find employment, making them particularly vulnerable. At the YMCA, we believe that extra help and support concerning access to services, supporting families and providing suitable accommodation could avert the breakdown of families and prevent young people from leaving home.

Youth homelessness: the facts

⇨ The breakdown of family relationships has been identified as the main cause of homelessness, often following years of family conflict and some violent and abusive situations. In a survey of 50 families affected by youth homelessness, 72% of parents believe that extra help could prevent family breakdown.

⇨ Social and economic disadvantage are also factors and young people who become homeless are often from marginalised backgrounds. Research shows that among those most likely to become homeless are young people who have had a troubled childhood, including parents with mental health problems, family upheaval and violence and abuse within the home. Self-harming, involving drugs, alcohol, crime and violence, are also behaviours linked with homelessness. Homelessness impacts upon the mental health and well-being of young people. A significant minority of young homeless people have complex needs.

⇨ Data on youth homelessness is limited and is based only on the numbers of young people who have sought help from agencies and service providers. There are many more hidden homeless who rely on extended family or friends to provide them with a floor, a sofa or a bed to sleep on.

⇨ Young people aged between 16 and 25 made up 39% of the total homeless population during 2005/06, based on Government figures for England. Of the 36,770 young people who were deemed to be statutorily homeless, 7,440 were aged 16 to 17 and 900 were aged 18 to 20 and had previously been in local authority care. Both these groups have priority needs under housing legislation.

⇨ To be classified as statutorily homeless, a young person has to apply to their local authority. A decision then depends on an assessment of their particular circumstances. If accepted as being statutorily homeless, the local authority is required to provide accommodation if it also judges them to be in priority need.

⇨ A UK-wide review of youth homelessness published in 2008 by the Joseph Rowntree Foundation showed that in England and Wales the number of young homeless has fallen over the previous three years but remained constant in Scotland and Northern Ireland.

⇨ Despite a fall in numbers in some parts of the UK, the same survey indicates that in the whole of the UK around 75,000 young people continue to be at risk and are in contact with homelessness services every year. This includes at least 31,000 additional young people not recognised as being statutorily homeless.

⇨ The number of young people sleeping rough on any one particular night is comparatively low but the aggregate number experiencing rough sleeping in any one year is much higher. This suggests that when homelessness begins, a young person may experience a period of rough sleeping before finding temporary housing.

⇨ In November 2006, Ruth Kelly, then Secretary of State for Communities and Local Government, CLG, announced a package of measures to further prevent and tackle youth homelessness and a commitment that by 2010, no 16- or 17-year-olds should be placed in bed and breakfast accommodation by a local authority under the homelessness legislation, except in an emergency.

⇨ The National Youth Homelessness Scheme was launched by CLG in 2007, since when the number of 16- and 17-year-olds accepted as homeless and subsequently placed in bed & breakfast accommodation in England has fallen.

YMCA

⇨ In 2006, with support from CLG, the YMCA launched the Step-In project to prevent teenage homelessness and provide safe accommodation for young people in crisis situations. Step-In projects include supported lodging schemes, school education projects, family support and mediation, easy-access housing advice, and work with the private rented sector. In their first year, Step-In projects helped 1,396 teenagers: 1,174 with early advice and education, 85 with family support and mediation and 137 with a safe place to live and support for the future.

The YMCA Sleep Easy

Every night YMCAs provide rooms and support for 7,000 young people who would otherwise have nowhere else to sleep. To mark Poverty and Homelessness Action Week, 18 YMCAs in England staged sponsored sleep out events, raising a total pledged amount of £115,000 for their work with young people. Next year's Sleep Easy will take place on Saturday 29 January 2011.

References

⇨ This factsheet draws information from two reports: *Youth Homelessness in the UK*, published in May 2008 by the Joseph Rowntree Foundation, the Centre for Housing Policy at the University of York and Centrepoint; *Breaking it Down: Developing Whole-Family Approaches to Youth Homelessness*, a study carried out by YMCA England and Croydon Housing Association for Young Single Homeless (CAYSH) which sought the views of 50 parents and carers of homeless teenagers. Where Government statistics are used these come from Communities and Local Government Policy Briefing 18, *Tackling Youth Homelessness*, published in March 2007 © Crown Copyright 2007.

⇨ The above information is reprinted with kind permission from the YMCA: visit www.ymca.org.uk for more.

© YMCA

Emily's life

Emily's (*name has been changed*) earliest memory of abuse was when she was five or six years old.

Emily was not fully aware of what was happening at that young age. There were no specific patterns, but the beatings would be worse when her father was drunk. As Emily got older the beatings got worse but neither her mother nor the authorities did anything to help:

'He would beat me real bad. I would go to the doctors; they could see what was happening to me but they did or said nothing so I continued to think that it was OK, that it was normal.'

Emily's life was on a downward cycle. Her school work was suffering and she had to see a psychiatrist to help her deal with some of her issues, but still nothing was being done to address her experiences at home. She became dependent on drugs trying to escape the problems she was facing. 'I started smoking cannabis, took ecstasy and tried cocaine.' Emily would continue to smoke cannabis for the next couple of years – 'At worst I was smoking £20–£30 worth a day. Friends would ask me where I was getting the money from. I couldn't tell them exactly. I could just get it – I didn't always pay.'

Emily tried to stay away from home as much as possible. In order to get away she was prepared to put herself in danger. 'I first slept on a park bench after my GCSEs. Sometimes I would sleep on buses – getting on night buses and staying on there all night long. After the second night on a park bench I decided to go home and have a fresh start.'

However, her father's abuse worsened and her relationship with her mother began to deteriorate too. When her father came to her school and threatened her in front of teachers and pupils, it was the first time in all the years of abuse that social services intervened.

In January last year Emily left home for good. Aged just 16, she was placed in a B&B for the next two months. 'My first night there was really weird. I had a kettle, some food from friends and a change of clothes. The first week that I was there I didn't realise that I was actually homeless.'

In the following weeks and months the reality became apparent to Emily: 'I became very depressed and I missed college.' The issues mounted. Emily had already had to drop some of her subjects but by this time she had to drop them all.

Then Emily was referred to Centrepoint and since arriving, she has started to get her life back on track. She is working hard at college and plans to go to university one day. She has grabbed opportunities with both hands. She has helped to organise 'Life Wise' workshops and has become involved in the Youth Educator Programme at Centrepoint, helping Centrepoint staff to improve the ways that they work with young people, championing their perspective in how the organisation can move forward.

Emily is finally in a position to be able to realise her potential.

Centrepoint isn't just about offering a homeless person a room or a house, it changes lives. It gives us new opportunities that we would not get otherwise. These opportunities are very valuable to young people. Some of us do not realise what we can achieve and ultimately we learn that we can do anything we want with our lives.

⇨ The above information is reprinted with kind permission from Centrepoint. Visit www.centrepoint.org.uk for more information.

© Centrepoint

Hidden homelessness

Information from Centrepoint.

It is very difficult to have a full picture of the numbers of young people who are homeless. Often single homeless young people exist out of sight due to 'sofa surfing' or staying with friends, or living in squats or hostels. Not all homeless young people approach their local council for help.

Every year the number of households in England who are accepted as homeless by their local authorities are counted by the Government. These figures include young people who are in priority need (those who find themselves homeless when they are 16 or 17 years old, or a care leaver up to the age of 21) or who are heads of families.

The Government statistics continue to report a fall in homelessness. The latest statistics, produced by Communities and Local Government, showed that six per cent of all the households accepted as homeless and in priority need through being a young person[1].

However, Centrepoint believes that there are several thousand young people who experience homelessness without having any contact with local authorities in England each year.

In 2004, Centrepoint worked with the University of York to estimate the total numbers of young homeless people (aged 16 to 24) in England. They estimated that there were between 36,000 and 52,000 'official' homeless young people – that is, those found to be homeless by the local authority – in a given year[2].

The most recent study conducted by the University of York and Centrepoint looking at youth homelessness across the UK estimates that at least 75,000 young people experience homelessness each year[3]. These are the young people we know about – it does not take into account those who are hidden homeless.

Rough sleeping

Recent analysis of the data available in London on the number of people who sleep rough indicates that eight per cent of rough sleepers on any given night are under the age of 25[4]. However, we know from our own evidence that young people have very different patterns of rough sleeping to adults and those who are more entrenched rough sleepers.

According to Centrepoint young people, and evidenced in the recent review of youth homelessness conducted by the University of York in partnership with Centrepoint[5], young people tend to sleep rough for shorter periods of time. Most young people describe sleeping rough for under one month – often just a few days – which they intersperse with sofa-surfing or staying with friends. However, this experience may occur many times before a young person finally secures temporary accommodation.

Young people are more likely to sleep rough in a variety of places where outreach services or street counts are unlikely to find them: on public transport, in parks, Internet cafes, private gardens or tower block bin rooms and stairs. In addition, young people at Centrepoint report that they deliberately sleep rough in hidden places for safety reasons, to avoid violence and drugs or to avoid being recognised by family or friends.

Around 50 per cent of young people who currently stay at Centrepoint have experienced rough sleeping prior to engaging in our services. Yet we know the majority of these young people have never been included in an official count. If young people have a fragmented pattern of sleeping rough, then they are less likely to be found by street outreach teams and they will continue to go under-represented in official statistics.

Notes

1 Statutory Homelessness: 4th Quarter (October to December) 2009, England, Communities and Local Government.

2 Centrepoint Youth Homelessness index: An estimate of youth homelessness for England, University of York, 2004.

3 Youth Homelessness in the UK, 2008. The report was commissioned by Centrepoint, conducted by the University of York and funded by the Joseph Rowntree Foundation.

4 Street to Home: Annual Report for London. 1st April 2008 to 31st March 2009, Broadway. This report is based on statistics from the CHAIN database.

5 Youth Homelessness in the UK, 2008.

⇨ Information from Centrepoint: www.centrepoint.org.uk

© Centrepoint

CENTREPOINT

Youth homelessness

You can be legally homeless if the place you live is unsafe, unsuitable or you have no legal right to be there. Before you leave home, find out about your housing rights and whether your local authority can help you find accommodation.

Leaving home and running away

There are a number of reasons that young people leave or run away from home. They may:

⇨ be getting away from violence or an abusive relationship with a family member;

⇨ have been thrown out by their parents or carers;

⇨ have lost their parents.

Because no-one under the age of 18 can sign a tenancy contract or mortgage agreement of their own, many homeless teens:

⇨ are forced to sleep on the street;

⇨ get friends to lend them a bed or sofa for the night;

⇨ stay with another family.

Once you're 18 years old, you have to apply to a local authority as being homeless to find out whether you qualify for housing

If you're in any of these situations, you'll be considered as officially homeless, so it's really important to find out what your options are.

Running away is a big risk and is usually not the best or safest way of dealing with things.

Housing rights for under-16s

If you're under 16, you can't make the decision to leave home yourself, as an adult will need to take responsibility for you.

If you are having serious problems at home, your local authority can:

⇨ help you sort things out with your parents;

⇨ arrange for you to live with another family member or adult, like a friend's parent;

⇨ find you emergency accommodation if you are worried about violence or abuse at home.

You'll also be able to talk to a social worker about why you think you need to leave home.

The social worker will try to work out if there's any way that you can return home. If living at home is too dangerous or impossible, they will look at other options including local authority care or living with a foster family.

Housing rights if you're 16 or 17

Almost all 16- and 17-year-olds are judged to be in 'priority need' when it comes to housing. This means the housing department of your local authority can help find you somewhere to live.

The exceptions are:

⇨ if you have lived abroad and are not a British citizen;

⇨ if you have spent at least 13 weeks in care since the age of 14;

⇨ if you are classed as a 'child in need'.

If any of these apply to you, then the social services department will deal with your case.

Social services will check your situation to see if there's any way you can return home, or go and live with another relative. They cannot force you to go back to anywhere you do not feel safe.

Housing rights if you're 18 or over

Once you're 18 years old, you have to apply to a local authority as being homeless to find out whether you qualify for housing.

Once you've completed your application, the authority will do a detailed investigation of your personal situation.

They will check:

⇨ whether you need emergency accommodation while your application is being looked at;

⇨ whether it's reasonable for you to stay in your current place;

⇨ whether your current accommodation suits your needs.

If your homelessness application is unsuccessful,

DIRECTGOV

your local authority will send you a letter that explains why.

Even if this is the case, they may be able to give you more help and advice on finding somewhere to live.

You may also be able to get financial help and benefit payments to help with your living costs.

Leaving foster or local authority care

If you're planning to move from foster or local authority care, the financial help and support you can get depends on a number of factors, including:

⇨ your age;

⇨ how long you have been in care;

⇨ how old you were when you went into care.

To make sure you get a full picture of your housing rights before you leave care, talk to your nearest housing advice centre.

Housing for young parents

If you're pregnant or already have children and you're worried about your housing situation, your local council will put you in 'priority need' of housing.

Organisations that can help with accommodation problems

Shelter

Shelter is a national charity that helps thousands of people every year with housing problems.

Although Shelter can't house you, Shelter advisers can point you in the right direction once they have assessed your situation.

They operate a free housing advice helpline (0808 800 4444) and have a website packed with detailed advice about a range of housing issues (shelter.org.uk/getadvice).

The Foyer Federation

The Foyer Federation runs 134 buildings called 'foyers' around the UK.

As well as offering homeless young people somewhere to stay, foyers are also a place where young people can support each other.

Living in a foyer also gives you access to learning, training and advice on how to find a job and live independently.

⇨ The above information is reprinted with kind permission from Directgov. Visit www.direct.gov.uk for more.

© Crown copyright

Young runaways

The statistics relating to young runaways make for a depressing read:

⇨ An estimated 100,000 children and young people run away each year in the UK for a wide variety of reasons such as physical, sexual, verbal or emotional abuse, neglect and peer pressure.

⇨ Children and young people in care are much more likely to have run away than those living at home. 45 per cent of young runaways are looked-after children.

⇨ One in seven children and young people rely on dangerous and risky strategies for survival such as stealing, begging and survival sex.

⇨ Runaways under the age of 16 are more likely to have other problems in their lives, including problems with depression, alcohol, drugs, offending, peer relationships and at school.

⇨ 25 per cent of runaways under 16 will sleep rough at some point and 15 per cent of them will get physically or sexually assaulted.

In response to these figures, local authorities and partner agencies respond to the needs of young runaways in a variety of ways to ensure a joined-up approach to supporting vulnerable children and young people. This includes developing joint guidance and multi-agency services to provide early intervention and family mediation support aimed at preventing children and young people from running away in the first place.

Emergency accommodation may also be required when a young runaway has been located by the police or local authority. It is often not possible and would be dangerous to expect some young runaways to return to the place where they had been living prior to running away. Therefore, it is important that local authorities ensure they have systems in place to safely accommodate young runaways whilst a longer term solution is found.

Young runaways ultimately require somewhere safe to go and need to know how to access that provision, so that they are not put at even greater risk. The two case studies linked to this theme highlight the innovative work being done in Manchester and West Sussex to support young runaways.

⇨ Information from the Department for Communities and Local Government: www.communities.gov.uk

© Crown copyright

DIRECTGOV / DEPARTMENT FOR COMMUNITIES AND LOCAL GOVERNMENT

Family breakdown to blame for youth homelessness

Information from Inside Housing.

By Emily Twinch

Family breakdown is the root cause of youth homelessness and is likely to increase as unemployment rises, according to research by Centrepoint.

The charity for homeless 16- to 25-year-olds found nearly two-thirds of young people who left home over the last year did so because of arguments and a breakdown in relationships.

Centrepoint chief executive Seyi Obakin said: 'Making the transition to adulthood is challenging for some young people. Equally, parenting teenagers can prove difficult for some adults, creating conflict in the family home.

'Yet too many families are not getting the support they need, when they need it. By the time a family conflict reaches crisis point, a focus on keeping young people at home is not necessarily the answer.'

The best remedy is early intervention, he added, and shifting the focus from the young person as the problem to supporting the family, including extended families.

60 homeless 16- to 25-year-olds were interviewed between December 2008 and March 2009 for the report, *Family life: the significance of family to homeless young people.*

It notes: 'Despite early signs of recovery in some areas of the economy, unemployment levels are continuing to rise which is likely to increase the stress and burden on families for many months to come.'

The research also found that although the majority of young people had some contact with their family, more than a fifth – 22 per cent – had no contact at all.

'Young people generally agreed there was a special bond between blood relations that meant they were more likely to be there for each other, but many felt that being family was also about treating each other well,' the report states.

'Blood relations could therefore lose "family" status, and step-parents or friends could become family if they cared for them and were always there.'

The main benefit of family for young people was knowing someone was always there to provide practical and emotional support, it also notes.

The vast majority of young people complained of frequent arguments, which were mainly caused by rebellious behaviour.

Half of the young people did not think family mediation services would help because they did not think their families would change, or could feel it was too intrusive.

The report suggests mentors and friendships can be supported to fill a void when young people cannot be reunited with their families.

25 November 2009

⇨ The above information is reprinted with kind permission from Inside Housing. Visit www.insidehousing.co.uk for more information.

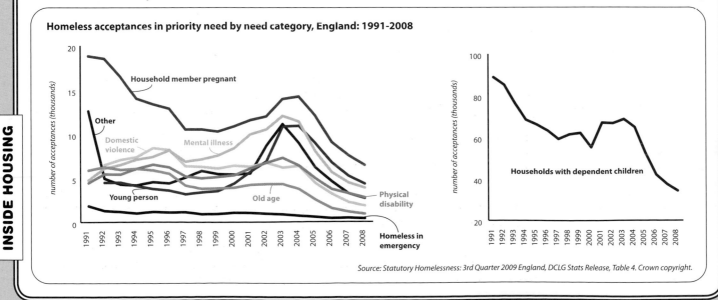

Homeless acceptances in priority need by need category, England: 1991-2008

Source: Statutory Homelessness: 3rd Quarter 2009 England, DCLG Stats Release, Table 4. Crown copyright.

INSIDE HOUSING

Off the radar

Children and young people on the streets in the UK.

Family and home

With few exceptions, the majority of the children and young people's experiences of family life were fraught with difficulties that they were often left to manage, with no explanation or support.

Many of the children and young people lived in single-parent families for all or part of their childhoods. Many lone mothers raised their children in challenging circumstances. Single mothers were less likely to abuse their children than mothers living with a partner.

Some children and young people have never met one of their parents and many lost contact with their fathers after parents separated. In a few cases, mothers left the family and broke contact with the child or young person.

Being lied to about the identity of their biological father often had negative consequences for a child or young person and their relationship with their mother, and played a part in becoming detached.

Children and young people often idealised absent or distant fathers and were not so critical of fathers' behaviours as they were of mothers who were often more involved in raising and caring for them.

Relationships with step-parents were often poor but there were also cases where children and young people spoke very highly of a step-parent.

Many children and young people did not have contact with their parent/s at the time of their participation in the research.

Grandparents played an important role in some children and young people's lives, caring for them when parents were unable to, but testing relationships with grandmothers, due to generational and cultural expectations, also led to children and young people becoming detached.

Many of the children and young people's parents experienced substance misuse, domestic violence and mental health issues. Often these issues led to parents being chaotic or emotionally unavailable and impacted upon their ability to care for their children. Parental issues were often a factor where there was abuse of children.

More than half of the children and young people experienced physical abuse, with fathers most frequently the perpetrator, despite the relatively low numbers of fathers involved with their children.

A small number of children and young people were sexually abused by step-relatives and by family friends.

One young person was subject to sexual abuse with the complicity of her mother.

Neglect and other forms of emotional abuse were commonly experienced.

The role of young carer was forced upon or adopted by some children and young people with consequences for their schooling and peer relationships.

The experiences of the children and young people with care-givers raise concerns about implications of them developing disorganised attachment. The children and young people's parents are also likely to have experienced negative parenting that prevented them from responding to their own children's needs in a positive manner.

A fifth of children and young people grew up in abject poverty. The majority lived in social housing in low-income families.

Over a quarter of all children and young people have become pregnant or fathered a child at a young age and only a couple of young females' children remained living with them. Most of the young fathers had emulated the patterns of many children and young people's own fathers by not having contact with their children. A couple of young fathers were unable to have contact with their children because of gang-related issues.

It was common for research participants to have experienced the premature death of a parent, often in disturbing circumstances, with profound impacts.

Secrets and lies were all too often part of family life with children and young people sometimes not telling a parent that they knew the truth about secrets kept from them and lies they had been told.

Violence

For many children and young people who participated in the research, violence was part of daily life in the home, in their local neighbourhood, at school and on the streets.

A few children and young people experienced violence in the care system at the hands of those charged with their care.

Violence also took the form of children and young people damaging property and experiencing threats and intimidation prior to becoming detached and once detached.

Young females experienced domestic violence in their relationships with older boyfriends. One young male also described perpetrating domestic violence.

Sexual violence was experienced by both young males and young females, including being gang-raped and being passed round by men for sex. Some sexual violence took place when children and young people were living on the streets.

Violence, in general, was a common experience on the streets, with children and young people being victims of violence, responding with violence in self-defence and perpetrating violence.

Carrying a knife was common amongst young males and a small number of young males carried and used guns.

Whilst the majority of the children and young people described hanging out with groups of others on the streets, approximately half of all young males self-defined as belonging to a gang. However, there was some diversity in children and young people's descriptions of a gang. Whilst many emulated elements of gang behaviour, few young males belonged to organised gangs with an identifiable order that were highly structured and involved in, for example, organised violence and the sale of guns and drugs. Territorial issues, to differing degrees, were apparent in gang activity. With one exception, those young males who self-identified as belonging to a gang were white. The few young females who self-defined as belonging to a gang were limited to groups of children, young people and adults who came together on the streets for general survival. All of the young males who experienced being part of more organised gangs had exited, or were seeking to exit, violence and gang association. Descriptions of gang life and reasons for joining gangs reveal the similarities between the process of becoming detached and being part of a gang, the nature of gangs and the important role gangs play in providing protection and an alternative to family.

From the description of the lives of the few young people who have left the streets and have a more settled life, it is apparent that violence continues to be a part of their lives.

For many of the children and young people who participated in the research, violence has often become normalised. Descriptions of their lives reveal how children and young people who are victims of violence become perpetrators after learning to respond with violence. Violence can become a currency whereby a child or young person protects themselves by being able to defend themselves and by ensuring their reputation for violence will act as a deterrent to others seeking to harm them. Violence may also serve as an outlet for bottled-up emotions relating to, for example, being abused, anger and frustration.

The streets

The majority of children and young people spent time on the streets prior to becoming detached, drawn to the streets because there was nothing for them at home and also because the streets offer freedom and fun.

Sometimes conflict arose between parents or carers and children and young people relating to what children and young people were doing on the streets. This conflict could act as the trigger for children and young people becoming detached and permanently on the streets.

As well as running away and being thrown out of home, children and young people also drifted to the streets.

Children and young people in care sometimes took to the streets because they were unhappy in their care placement or wanted to be with particular people.

Prior to becoming detached, integration with homeless communities could hasten the speed at which a child or young person took to the streets and became detached.

The homeless community could be a source of support and protection as well as a risk to children and young people. Some children and young people sought out others on the streets but others actively avoided the homeless community, viewing homeless adults as different and as a potential danger.

Neglect and other forms of emotional abuse were commonly experienced [by children and young people on the streets in the UK]

With a couple of exceptions, those children and young people who did not sleep on the streets were street-involved.

Children and young people employed a number of survival strategies on the streets including shoplifting, burglary, stealing cars, involvement in selling drugs, selling sex and begging and blagging. Sometimes spending time with others on the streets was an invaluable source of support. Survival strategies also entailed identifying safe places to be and practising attitudes and behaviour to minimise danger.

Some children and young people viewed their time on the streets as wholly negative whilst others described it as being largely positive.

For some, being on the streets was normal because it was experienced by many of their peers. It appears to be difficult to withdraw from street life, even when a young person has permanent accommodation.

3 November 2009

⇨ The above information is an extract from The Railway Children's report *Off the Radar*, and is reprinted with permission. Visit www.railwaychildren.org.uk for more.

© The Railway Children

No place like home

A cockroach-infested flat one week, a cold room in a cramped hostel the next. Incredibly, this is how 130,000 children in Britain live today.

By Louise Carpenter

Six months ago, Billy-Jo, a 29-year-old single mother, was evicted with her four children from their home after her violent partner smashed in the windows. He had often hit her before, too – 18 times the police came – but she always refused to prosecute. She had to leave because of the damage and threw herself on the mercy of Greenwich Council, but they suggested that without court proceedings she was regarded as having made herself intentionally homeless and that she could provide no proof that she was a good tenant. That she had four children under the age of 11, the youngest being one, and nowhere to live, was irrelevant in her application for a council house. Her children's welfare came under the care of social services, and while she has a social worker looking after the interests of Karl, 11, Shane, ten, Rosie, five, and Ronnie, one, there is never any interaction between housing and social services departments. Whatever the circumstances, a housing application can never be made to a housing department on behalf of children – a nationwide policy which seems extraordinary given the aims of the Government's Green Paper of 2003, 'Every Child Matters'.

The issue of homelessness is often imbued with implicit moralising. Whether it be to do with drink, drugs or prostitution, it's easy to think the homeless have brought it on themselves. In our mind's eye, the homeless are always grown-up, or at least half grown-up; men sleeping in boxes under bridges or swigging spirits on park benches; women on the game, funding smack habits; teenage runaways searching for escape, for answers. Who thinks about babies? Toddlers? Children who might be sitting next to ours in primary schools, many of whom miss a quarter of their education because of the upheaval?

According to Barnardo's, there are 52,250 homeless families in London and another 20,000 throughout the UK. Of these, 73% involve minors, putting the overall estimate of homeless children at more than 130,000, a figure accepted by the Government but treated with caution by Shelter, the homelessness charity. Those 130,000 are just the ones for whom local councils have accepted responsibility. There are thousands more who have not yet made it to a statistic but have no place they can call home.

Research on these children makes for grim reading: a third have no fixed school because they are frequently moved from hostels to houses to flats by councils juggling demand; they have no doctor, no place to play, no single social worker who can ensure they do not slip through the net (Victoria Climbié was in temporary accommodation). They live in hostels or former B&Bs for months on end. They experience shame, rejection, fear, stress, anger. They are bullied and called names like 'pikey' and 'scab'. Unlike in Ken Loach's 1966 film *Cathy Come Home*, children are rarely confiscated now, although it remains a risk.

For every statistic, or non-statistic, there is a real child who is trying to cope. It is because of this that Billy-Jo and the children and three other families agreed to feature in a BBC five-part documentary series, *Sofa Surfers*, about child homelessness, to be aired on CBBC next week – part of a homelessness season on CBBC aimed at breaking down prejudices, especially among children themselves. The series explores the day-to-day reality; the children's hopes, their dreams, their disappointments. But, more than anything else, it shows their bravery, a heartbreaking acceptance of circumstances over which they have no control.

Billy-Jo opens the front door of her emergency house. She wears earrings, rings and heavy kohl around her eyes, and has a steely look that seems to encapsulate years of trouble and disruption that began long before her children were born. In the past six months, before arriving in Belvedere, a grim place just beyond south-east London, Billy-Jo and the children have been moved five times in and out of emergency flats and houses, sometimes for as little as two days at a time, and often far from their schools.

When she complained about her three-hour daily commute to the primary school, navigating trains and buses with her buggy, she was told bluntly, 'Change their schools.' She refused to do it, pointing out that she might well be moved again, and recognising education as the single source of stability in her children's increasingly peripatetic and chaotic lives.

A decision has not yet been reached about whether or not the family will qualify for council accommodation. So they are here in a soulless house with lorries thundering past, one of thousands of houses and flats on lease to the council from private landlords charging massive rents, picked up by housing benefit, and usually of poor quality. 'They told me I was lucky,' Billy-Jo tells me. She goes on to explain that when they moved in, the place was infested with cockroaches and parasites. They have had mice under the fridge, mould in the bathroom, leaks in the kitchen. There are bare bulbs, curtains hanging off poles and piles of washing everywhere. What toys she was allowed to grab quickly are stacked in Pampers boxes. Clothes dry

THE GUARDIAN

on radiators. She is not allowed to pin up pictures, so here and there are odd photos of her children, propped up on 1970s-style gas fires.

She points to a hole in the sitting room floor and tells me she thinks the previous person unlucky enough to fetch up here must have had a Staffordshire bull terrier that took a chunk out of the wood with its teeth. Her furniture is in storage until a final decision is made and so nothing here belongs to them, not even the quilts or the bedding.

Just when I feel myself sinking under the weight of the grimness of Billy-Jo's life, the children charge into view and lighten the mood. Shane has vacuumed the room he shares with his brother especially for my visit. 'He loves order,' Billy-Jo says, 'he's a very proud little boy.' Shane tells me he wanted his room to be clean and tidy, even though he hates it because the beds are uncomfortable and the window blows a draught that stops him from sleeping properly. Karl reveals that one day he will be a footballer – 'I will live in a four-bedroom mansion with my girlfriend, not my wife: a piece of paper changes nothing.' Rosie, a sweet five-year-old, is doing well with her reading – her teacher calls her 'my little ray of sunshine'.

I go up to Shane and Karl's room with them. There isn't much there, bar a chest of drawers and two beds. They have their games console with them, but not much else.

During 2009, nearly 65,000 households were found to be homeless in England

The council wouldn't even let them get out their Christmas tree for Christmas Day because it was packed away in a council storage container. Billy-Jo helped them paint a tree on some paper instead, which they decorated with tinsel.

'I feel angry because the council can't be bothered to give us a proper home, without cockroaches or mice,' says Shane. 'I just want a tidy room, nice and warm – and comfy beds.' And your friends? Would you play with them here after school? He looks puzzled, like I've suggested we fly to the moon.

I know that Shane feels he is being bullied at school, although he doesn't admit it to me at first: 'I see them pointing at me and then they start laughing,' he says, staring into the camera. 'I am trying to fit in, but it's not working. My friends hate me.' I wander into Rosie's room: 'I want a pink room,' she says, looking at the horrid brown curtains, 'and my Disney box. I have to have the door open at night now because I don't like the dark.'

The family lives under strict rules laid down by the management company, which have been framed in cheap

pine as if to enforce the point: No visitors after 9pm; Spot checks anytime from 8am to 9pm; No washing machine or tumble dryer use. 'Social services said to me: "Make sure their uniforms are clean",' Billy-Jo tells me. 'But I said, "How am I supposed to wash their clothes? I'm not allowed to use the washing machine".' Billy-Jo has no idea why she is not allowed to use the washing machine, but does anyway, for the children, putting it on double spin because that's the only way it works.

The burden on Billy-Jo is enormous. Later, when I do the school run with her, I can hardly believe she manages. She's on and off buses with all four children, each with their own demands. 'I just need to be settled again,' she says, suddenly seeming young. 'I feel like I am being punished for the damage to the house, but it wasn't my fault. It went to court, compensation was paid. Why do me and the children still have to suffer?'

She has a point. The stress of her housing situation is one of the biggest problems in her life. It seems ironic that on top of all the old problems that caused her family to be homeless in the first place, they now have a newer, more immediate problem that has arisen from a failure by administrators to see the bigger picture, to understand how housing bureaucracy will test Billy-Jo's children even more.

Adam Sampson, former chief executive of the homelessness charity Shelter, confirms this. 'There is a bureaucratic gap between providing housing and social services, which only have the children's welfare in mind. Decisions are never made with a holistic view of what a family needs. And yet housing is right at the centre of a child's welfare and it is only recently that Government departments are recognising that. It is emotionally devastating for a child to be in this position but, to be fair to officers, there is now a massive shortage of housing, a pressure from the Government to get people into private leasing agreements. Added to that, because of the credit crunch the number of new homes being built will drop dramatically, adding further pressure to an already overstretched and increasingly unaffordable housing market.'

Hence, the whole process appears to be a game of tactics, with council officers playing with a depleted housing stock and increasing applications. 46,000 homes were repossessed during 2009; the number is estimated to reach 53,000 this year.

Shelter has worked closely with the Government on its own 'Keys to the Future' policy, designed to help thousands of children by 2011. There are two things desperately needed to solve the problem: the first is children being taken into account in the processing of housing applications, of families being considered as human beings rather than statistics. The second is nothing short of a massive building programme of affordable homes.

In 2007, 380 council houses were completed along with 26,860 new 'units' of social housing (mostly housing

THE GUARDIAN

association property). In the 60s and 70s, this figure was above 100,000. Barnardo's believes the current rate should at the very least be doubled, if not brought into line with what it has been in the past. The lack of houses is the reason why homeless families applying for housing are moved so much. Priority needs are measured on a points system and each council is going for the big prize, which is rejecting as many applications as it can and shuffling families into the private sector, funded by housing benefit, where they will no longer be a homeless statistic and have a right to a home for life.

There are thousands more [homeless children] who have not yet made it to a statistic but have no place they can call home

But that still leaves the children with no one to help them but their parents. According to John Reacroft, children's services manager of the Barnardo's Families in Temporary Accommodation Project, it is seeing their parents' stress and anger that often gets to the children the most. They hate seeing their parents fight, and their mothers cry. They want to wipe away these adult tears, so much more upsetting than their own. There is a heartbreaking moment in the film where Shane looks at the camera and says, 'I have got a happy life. I love my mum. I said to her that I wanted to marry her, and she said, "You can't".' He pauses, and then adds, 'But I would if I could.'

A week later, I am on the other side of London, near Haringey, which, after Victoria Climbié and Baby P, has become a byword for child poverty and neglect. It is 7am and I am waiting to be let into a hostel for homeless families – a brown Victorian building that looks like an ex-army barracks. It sits behind a fence and, in the reception area, CCTV cameras reveal small corridors snaking round corners, off which are communal kitchens.

I am reminded of what Billy-Jo was told by the council, that she was lucky to have a house at all, and looking at this hulk of a building providing 100 families with emergency accommodation, living cheek by jowl, I can see why the council told her she was lucky. Hostels are at the bottom of the pile when it comes to emergency housing. According to Nuala Sharkey, advice and advocacy worker for the Finsbury Park Homeless Families Project, who is trying to help the family I am about to see, homeless children are rarely so because of their parents' drink and drug habits. For most, it is a complicated web of social reasons: a death in the family; arrears; unprosecuted domestic violence; a simple lack of money.

In the case of Amanda, 14, and Daniel, 11, it was the collapse of their father's business. They enjoyed a millionaire lifestyle while living in the States, but now they are penniless. Their father, who has a British passport, has brought them to the UK to try to rebuild his family's life.

Their mother and sisters remain in Nigeria, waiting to be brought over. Nuala Sharkey, who is chasing the housing application, is pessimistic: 'They have a house in Nigeria,' she says with a sigh. 'I'm almost sure they'll be rejected.' So what will happen to the children? 'They'll have to throw themselves at the mercy of social services, under section 17 of the Children's Act, which says children have a right to be housed. They would then go through the rent deposit scheme where social services provide one month's deposit and then one month's rent, but then they are on their own, relying on housing benefit.'

Human rights laws will protect a parent from losing a child through homelessness, but if the parent is rejected by a housing department, social services is the only recourse and the very application itself makes a child being taken into care a technical possibility. 'Usually, in the case of a migrant, they might offer a ticket back to where the family came from,' Sharkey says.

I wander through the corridors looking for their twin rooms – Daniel and his father John in one, Amanda in another. Children's shoes are piled up outside doors, High School Musical trainers and slippers, and flip-flops. Daniel comes out first. He is a happy boy, only just arrived in the hostel from foster care in Ireland. The reality of the situation does not seem to have sunk in. 'We are not homeless,' he tells me. 'My dad is doing his best and will have another business soon. He used to buy me 20, 30, 40 movies... and trainers and shoes.' He says he wants to be an astronaut: 'You can be homeless on the moon if your space shuttle breaks down.' In the film, he builds a house out of Lego and identifies himself as the man in front watering his garden.

Amanda is far more closed. She does not let me see her room, which I know is identical to that shared by her brother and father, small with an iron single bed and a brown cupboard. Her hair is gelled and she wears lipgloss, which she sucks and licks in nervousness. We sit next to one another on the bus on the way to her school, she texting her friends with expert glittered fingertips, me silent beside her. She is a teenager missing her mother, living in the most awful hostel conditions: 'I am trying to cope,' she tells me eventually.

When she gets a text saying her mate is downstairs, she leaps up, the first burst of energy I have seen. She greets her friend, who has no idea of her homelessness, with a wide smile. There begins a long conversation about Facebook. Amanda's father is against her virtual world, but it strikes me that it must be better than the one she lives in right now.

Mel is unlike the other children I have met. Perhaps it is because her problems have been going on for longer, and

THE GUARDIAN

that she has hit the difficult age of 13, but the damage seems deeper. She was made homeless with her family after an arson attack on her house. She has been excluded from school and is now in a part-time pupil referral unit. She hates school and seems wary of adults. She lives in North Wales with her mother and siblings, protected by an extraordinary project called Save the Family, set up by a former nursery teacher, Edna Speed, now in her eighties, to help homeless families where there is a real risk that the children will be taken into care.

Save the Family houses 24 families in a series of converted farm buildings. They have 70 applications a month but can only accept three, usually cases where the children are most at risk, most traumatised. When Mel and her siblings arrived, she tells me that she was suicidal: 'When I first got here, there was lots going on and I felt like killing myself,' she says. 'But I feel OK, I have people helping me. I just needed somebody to talk to but I didn't know who.' She tells me about her youth worker, Georgie: 'I can trust her,' she says. 'That's a new feeling for me.'

The charity is funded by donations, Government grants and the housing benefit to which each family is entitled. It provides a roof over each family's head, a safe place to be for around five months until they can get themselves back on their feet. There are extra classes for children falling behind, a theatre, a nursery, support staff to help parents get through the most traumatic time of their life and youth workers for every child, who will sort out problems with school or authorities: 'Often the parent is so worn down or frightened of authority themselves, that we find it helpful if we step in as a protection,' explains Tim McLachlan, the charity's chief executive. It offers precisely what campaigners believe is so lacking elsewhere: a holistic view of the families, an approach where children are seen as people rather than a housing irrelevance.

Amy Hulley, now 18, was a resident there more than ten years ago, after she became homeless with her mother and brother following a traumatising break-up from her father, who was diagnosed a paranoid schizophrenic. She remembers children at school calling her names. 'Not all the time,' she says, 'but it always came up in an argument because we'd arrive in this Save the Family minibus and I'd always try and get him to park it round the corner.' Still, she got extra tuition because she'd missed so much school. In time, her mother finally got herself back on her feet. Amy is now a talented actress and being encouraged to try for RADA: 'I didn't even know what the theatre was until I got to Save the Family. Not only did it give us a home, and got me back on track with my schooling, but it changed my life.'

Her optimism reminds me of 12-year-old Sagal, whose mother, Abshiro, a quiet, dignified woman, came to the UK with her two children, fleeing the violence in Somalia. I meet her in a café around the corner from Amanda and Daniel's hostel. Living in temporary accommodation in north London, Abshiro and her children do not have the support of Save the Family and yet they seem to be living by the same beliefs, the same conviction that one day they will overcome their situation and achieve a better life.

Sagal, by coincidence, attends the same school as Amanda. In addition, every Sunday evening Abshiro uses her benefits to pay for two hours of tutoring for her daughter, who one day intends to become a doctor.

When I talk to Sagal, she tells me: 'Doctors save people, don't they? I want to save lives, help people's suffering. I really am trying very hard. I have my mum, and with her I feel safe and secure. I don't mind that we don't have a home. We are best friends and I love her very much and I know she loves me.' I ask her where she wants to live finally, when she is a doctor: 'America, in California or Florida,' she says. Why there? 'Because there are so many beaches and it is always sunny,' she replies. It is a dream of escape, a sunny yellow brick road that will one day lead her away from the poverty of Seven Sisters Road.

As part of the documentary, Billy-Jo, Shane, Karl, Rosie, Ronnie, Amanda, Daniel, their father John, Abshiro, Sagal and her four-year-old brother Mahad travel to North Wales for a weekend break at Save the Family. In the week after they return, I visit Billy-Jo and the children. Billy-Jo appears perkier and the children happy: 'I was so trodden down before I went,' she says, 'I was convinced I was going to crack. But you know, those few days away and I feel recharged again.'

She tells me she is going to try to find a lawyer who might help her case (six hours can be provided through legal aid). I see some brightly coloured sweet wrappers pinned on a corkboard by the kitchen: 'Me and Rosie ate those snuggled up in bed together in Wales,' she explains.

I'm glad Billy-Jo kept her sweet wrappers. They are a reminder of happier times, a talisman of hope for the future, solid proof that there are some things that can never be taken away.

The following apology was printed in the Observer's For the record column, Sunday 22 March 2009.

This article was wrong to state that 'there is never any interaction' between the housing and social services departments of Greenwich Council. We accept that there is ongoing, extensive liaison between them. The article also said the council had 'thousands of houses and flats on lease [for the homeless] from private landlords'. This is untrue. Greenwich has fewer than 300 homeless households in temporary accommodation. We apologise for these errors.

⇨ This article first appeared in the Observer, 8 March 2009

THE GUARDIAN

Work and skills

Information from Crisis.

Lack of work is a major cause and consequence of homelessness, eroding skills and self-esteem and acting as a practical obstacle to finding and keeping a home. Training and education can give homeless people the skills and confidence required to get them back on track and help them prepare for, find and keep jobs.

Low levels of skills and high levels of worklessness persist amongst the homeless population and despite investment in mainstream welfare to work programmes and interventions for low skilled adults, they do not work for the majority of homeless people who need more tailored support.

Work

Not having a job can lead to you losing your home and not having a home can seriously harm your chances of finding a job. Most homeless people have multiple labour market disadvantages and almost all have extremely low employability.

⇨ Only 2% of homeless people are in full-time employment. 12% work part-time. 13% do voluntary work.

⇨ 57% of homeless people have been unemployed for three years or more.

With an employment rate of 15%, homeless people are five times less likely than the wider population to be in employment. However, the vast majority of homeless people want to work either now (77%) or in the future (97%).[1]

Homeless people or those at risk of homelessness, ex-offenders, those with mental health needs, people who have alcohol/substance misuse issues and those with a past history of long or frequent benefit claims are amongst those likely to have additional support needs and to require extra support on their journey back to work.

Skills

Many homeless people have low or no qualifications and lack the necessary skills for sustained employment. Many have had bad experiences of formal education and find that mainstream adult learning doesn't cater for their needs. As a result they lose essential self-confidence and lack purpose for improving their prospects.

⇨ 60% of homeless people have low or no qualifications, putting over 80% of job vacancies beyond reach.

⇨ And 37% of homeless people have no qualifications whatsoever.

Only 2% of homeless people are in full-time employment

Even for those homeless people who have previously achieved qualifications and/or had successful jobs, the experience of homelessness itself deskills and isolates, destroying confidence, self-esteem and social ties. Many are caught in a destructive cycle of unemployment, mental health problems, addiction or reoffending, which prevents them taking control of their lives and moving on. Engaging in activity and learning and developing new skills is a way of breaking this cycle and many homeless people prefer learning in the more relaxed environments of voluntary settings such as the services Crisis provides.

Gaining new skills is not just a means of getting homeless people into employment. It builds confidence, gives structure to the day and a sense of purpose and achievement, improves mental health and well-being and gives people the tools to sustain a tenancy. Attending classes and training courses also provides the opportunity for social interaction, a chance to meet new people and make new friends. Investing in learning and skills projects for homeless people can therefore have multiple benefits for individuals, Government policy and public spending.

Notes

1   OSW (2005) *No Home, No Job.*

⇨ The above information is reprinted with kind permission from Crisis. Visit the charity's website at www.crisis.org.uk for more information on this and other related topics.

© Crisis

CRISIS

Homelessness prevention

Shelter's work centres around preventing homelessness, both through our critical support services for people in housing need, and our campaigns to improve Government policies and services for homeless people.

We believe people should not be allowed to become homeless, and that to properly tackle the issue of homelessness, its root causes need to be addressed.

The Government's approach to preventing homelessness

The 2002 Homelessness Act brought in new requirements for local authorities to assess and prevent homelessness in their local areas, and marked the start of a renewed Government focus on homelessness prevention.

New housing applicants are now typically required to participate in an initial 'housing options' interview. This involves a discussion of ways in which their immediate housing need could be met. Sometimes this means that no homelessness application is made. For instance:

⇨ young people who have been living with family or friends and have been asked to leave may be offered mediation with a view to enabling them to return;

⇨ people who experience domestic violence are offered 'sanctuary schemes', involving the installation of security measures within the home;

⇨ young people leaving the family home may be offered supported lodgings schemes where members of the community provide a room as temporary respite accommodation;

⇨ a significant part of this new preventative approach involves referring households to the private rented sector, often facilitating the move through payment of rent deposits;

⇨ local authorities will also provide general housing advice on available services, housing options, housing benefit and rent arrears.

Shelter's view

The 'housing options' approach

Shelter strongly supports the provision of a wider range of housing choices to those in difficulty. However, it is vital that the provision of such options does not prevent people from accessing their legal rights under homelessness law. Where there is a legal duty for local authorities to accept a homelessness application and provide temporary accommodation, households must be free to decide whether this is what they want, regardless of any other options that may have been identified.

The need for tenancy sustainment services

In many cases, advice alone is not sufficient to prevent homelessness. People in housing need often have significant problems – such as poor health, alcohol and drug misuse, and financial instability – that make it difficult for them to keep a tenancy and can result in recurring homelessness.

Shelter strongly supports the provision of a wider range of housing choices to those in difficulty

---

Shelter believes that every local authority should have a tenancy sustainment service to help people, particularly those forced to use the private rented sector, with the practicalities of moving into their new home and maintaining their tenancy.

Boosting legal aid

Shelter believes that funding for civil legal aid should be increased to enable those facing possession proceedings to access independent legal advice.

The need for earlier interventions and more affordable housing

While Shelter welcomes support services to prevent people in crisis from losing their homes, we believe that if the Government is serious about preventing homelessness then more needs to be done at an earlier stage to stop people falling into crisis in the first place. In particular, better ongoing support needs to be made available for those who need it, and more affordable housing must be made available in areas where demand currently outstrips supply.

Shelter calls on the Government to build more social rented housing and to provide specialist supported housing for those who need it.

This content applies to England only.

⇨ Information supplied by Shelter. For more details, visit shelter.org.uk

© Shelter

Why giving to those who beg does more harm than good

Information from Thames Reach.

'Don't be mean, you heard the man. How can you deny him a few pence for a cup of tea?'

Overwhelming evidence shows that people who beg on the street do so in order to buy hard drugs, particularly crack cocaine and heroin. These highly addictive drugs cause an extreme deterioration in people's health and even death.

This evidence comes from a number of sources. Firstly our outreach teams who are out and about on the streets of the capital working with London's homeless 365 days of the year. They estimate that 80 per cent of people begging do so to support a drug habit.

Secondly, when the police did some drug testing of people arrested for begging in Westminster in 2005, the figures indicated that seven in ten people tested positive for Class A drugs (crack cocaine or heroin). In a similar exercise carried out in Camden, 80 per cent tested positive for Class A drugs.

The evidence that the overwhelming majority of people begging on the streets of central London spend their begging money on crack cocaine and heroin is indisputable.

'Alright, but what about this chap? He's just a few pounds short of what he needs to book into a hostel tonight.'

The hostel accommodation set aside for London's homeless men and women does not require payment in order to 'book in'. Hostel rent is covered through Housing Benefit, which hostel workers can help the new resident to claim once they have moved into the hostel.

There are around 3,000 bed-spaces of hostel accommodation in London, which can be accessed via the street outreach teams that work in the central London boroughs. London Street Rescue, run by Thames Reach, is one of the main providers of outreach services across London. Our teams not only help people to find accommodation but also get them into drug and alcohol treatment mental health programmes. Outreach teams are active at night, and often during the day, seven days a week. Last year they helped over 400 people off the streets of the capital.

However, only 40 per cent of people arrested for begging in Westminster in 2005 claimed to be homeless. Most people begging have accommodation of sorts, either a hostel place or a flat or bedsit.

Most people who beg have accommodation. Outreach workers can help those who don't to access a hostel bed.

'Maybe, but there's surely no harm in giving a few pence.'

Giving to people who beg is not a benign act without consequences. As an organisation that has worked with people on the street for over twenty years, we have seen many lives damaged by hard drugs and alcohol misuse. We have even lost people through overdoses in situations where a significant portion of the money they spent on drugs came from members of the public giving loose change.

By all means, engage with people on the street. Perhaps buy them food or a cup of tea. Best of all, if you are concerned for them because you think they are sleeping rough, contact London Street Rescue.

Giving to people who beg is not a benign act. It can have fatal consequences.

'Come on, these are just people a bit down on their luck.'

Most people begging are not individuals in temporary difficulties, but people who are dependent on a begging income. This is almost certainly to fund a serious drug habit.

There is no need to beg on the streets in 2008. It is an urban myth that if you have no address, you cannot claim

THAMES REACH

benefits. This simply isn't true. Meanwhile, there are many day centres where homeless people can get food, clothing and support.

That is not to say that there are not many people on the streets needing help and support. Our London Street Rescue service is out every night, in search of the isolated rough sleepers who are missed by other services, helping them into accommodation and to find a way out of homelessness.

Many people asking for your money are caught up in a desperate cycle of begging from the public, 'scoring' drugs from a dealer and then taking these drugs.

There are many services seeking to help people sleeping rough. Please work with them, not against them.

'I'm half convinced, but surely if you don't give to people who beg then they will only turn to crime to fund their drug or alcohol addiction.'

It is something of a counsel of despair to think that we would give our loose change to people begging to stop them committing crime. Besides, the evidence does not bear out this proposition.

In 2003, police in Westminster and Camden made numerous arrests for begging, leading to the dispersal of regular beggars and an overall reduction in the number of people begging on the street. The police analysis that followed 'showed no displacement into crime by beggars moving off the street. The crime figures for Camden are down and Westminster's remain the same.'

For hostel residents who persist in begging, a reduction in the income supplied through begging can be the catalyst that leads them to spend more time working with staff and thinking about the future. This makes it easier for them to move on to more long-term accommodation or appropriate treatment, and away from the street.

There is no evidence that reducing begging leads to more crime. In fact, it can stimulate people to address their real needs, instead of avoiding facing them.

'Isn't this just about the councils wanting cleaner neighbourhoods?'

Thames Reach's primary concern is that people with serious drug and alcohol problems are gravely damaging their health and even putting their lives at risk using money raised through begging. However, we are also aware that local communities are justifiably concerned at the impact of begging on their neighbourhoods.

Research commissioned by the Home Office found that 54 per cent of the public choose not to use a cash point if there is someone begging next to it. These are reasonable fears that individual members of the public experience.

As a responsible organisation working with and in local communities, we seek to understand and address these concerns.

Working with communities to address concerns about begging and its impact is a responsibility that we at Thames Reach take very seriously.

'OK, you may have some valid points, but aren't you demonising all homeless people as feckless beggars and drug addicts?'

The main point we want to make is that the link is primarily between begging and the misuse of hard drugs, not between homelessness and begging or homelessness and drug misuse.

Most people sleeping rough do not beg and most people begging do not sleep rough. Although there are many rough sleepers with serious drug problems (we estimate that 40 per cent of the rough sleepers we help have a drug problem), the majority have not. Our overriding concern is to save lives. Every year there are drug or drink-related deaths amongst the homeless population on the street. Recent figures from an eminent doctor working with London's drug-using population indicated that the average age that intravenous drug users were dying in central London was shockingly only 31. We want to help people to get off the street and into decent accommodation where they can get the care and support they need. To do this we need the backing of the public.

The link is between begging and drug misuse, not homelessness and begging, nor even homelessness and drugs.

'OK, you've convinced me, how can I help people to get off the street and away from the dealers?'

Support local homelessness charities that are working with people in need. The best way of finding out about your local homelessness services is through Homeless London. Alternatively, you can donate directly to Thames Reach.

Finally, we are not asking you to just 'walk on by'. By all means engage street homeless people in conversation, even buy them a cup of tea or food. But please don't give them money. We have seen too many people die from overdoses on the street. Your kindness could kill.

There are plenty of ways of ensuring that your money is spent on finding real solutions to homelessness and drug and alcohol addiction. Help Thames Reach to end street homelessness.

⇨ Information from Thames Reach. Visit www. thamesreach.org.uk for more information.

© Thames Reach

THAMES REACH

The Big Issue celebrates its 18th birthday

Exactly 18 years on from the launch of the Big Issue, this radical street paper is still offering a vital lifeline for homeless people.

Billie Bickley is at her pitch in Covent Garden, grinning at her dog Solo. It is 9.30 on a bright, fresh morning, and she has already sold two-dozen *Big Issue*s to a steady flow of regular customers. Banter streams from her mouth, interspersed by commands that control Solo's ball-chasing acrobatics. 'Is that coffee for me?' she calls to a woman hurrying out through the doors of Pret A Manger.

'Billie's a legend round here,' says the woman, Melissa Bacon, 33, a market researcher who works nearby. 'She's always got a smile.' She hands Billie her coffee. 'We're all very proud of her.'

You could say that Bickley sells outside Pret A Manger, but locals know it's the other way round. 'Billie attracts customers to Pret,' one of the waitresses says. 'She knows everyone by name. While they're there talking to Billie, they decide to get a coffee.'

At one point, Pret offered Bickley a job – but there was a problem. 'I've got 96 convictions,' she says, looking up sheepishly. 'I didn't know until they looked at my record. I thought maybe I had 30 or something.' She warms her hands on her coffee. 'I'm 36, and for 17 years I was addicted to heroin. Nearly half my life. The *Big Issue*'s the only one that's trusted me with a job.'

It is 18 years this week since Gordon Roddick, who with his wife Anita ran the Body Shop, came up with the idea for a UK street paper. In 1991, at the height of the homelessness crisis, Roddick had seen a street paper on sale in New York, where he was looking at premises for the Body Shop. 'Near Grand Central Station, I passed a tall, black homeless guy who was selling a newspaper,' Roddick remembers. 'I was immediately interested in the interaction with his customers. He was laughing and joking. He wasn't invisible like the homeless people on the streets of London.'

The only thing that troubled Roddick was that homeless people were being given that paper for free. A pioneer of social business, he thought selling it to the homeless instead might end what he saw as a disempowering and dehumanising cycle of charity. He came back inspired, and asked the Body Shop Foundation to look into the idea of a street paper. 'They came back saying "it's too dangerous – there's an insurance issue, the police won't let you, the local authorities won't let you..." I thought to hell with it.'

But instead of abandoning the idea, Roddick called up his old friend John Bird, an ex-rough sleeper, ex-offender and poet he had met when they drank in the same Edinburgh pub 20 years earlier. 'John was the ideal person,' Roddick says. 'He'd worked in the printing industry. He'd been on the streets. He was very bright. He certainly wouldn't listen to what anyone would tell him he couldn't do.'

Roddick remembers with a laugh how his late wife and John used to fight. 'I liked it,' he says, 'it gave me some peace. If a notion was important enough, John and Anita were very similar in their entire disregard for other people as they pushed it through. I never had that quality and I admired it.'

Today, despite the recession, circulation is holding steady with a weekly sale of 147,000 copies, offering legitimate self-employment to 2,500 people in the UK. It is not a charity handout; vendors buy the magazine for 75p and sell it for £1.50. 'I hate hearing that people have given money and not taken the magazine,' Roddick says. 'I always give the vendor exactly £1.50, or ask for the change. I suspect John does exactly the same.'

Bickley was on the streets four years before the *Big Issue* existed, escaping a violent home at 14 for London. 'I got the first train from Coventry, got off at King's Cross and I've been here ever since,' she says. Within her

THE GUARDIAN

first week of living on the street, she was befriended by a homeless couple who sold heroin. 'The first time I took it was 17 June 1987, my 15th birthday. I kept on taking it for 17 years.'

It is 18 years since Gordon Roddick came up with the idea for a UK street paper

By the time Bickley was 21, she was also addicted to crack cocaine. 'I remember walking through King's Cross one day,' she says. 'Crack had just come out, and the dealers were hiding the drugs in their mouths. Right next to me, this guy's head gets blown off in the street by another dealer. There was blood all over my face – but I didn't care, I just wanted the crack that had been blown out of his mouth. I was picking up all the rocks off the street out of the blood and guts.'

An odd Bird

Sitting in a cafe in King's Cross, the centre of Bickley's world for 17 years, Bird says he initially refused the job Roddick offered him. 'I said no because I wasn't the slightest bit interested in charity.' He only agreed to look into it because Roddick offered him £100 a day, 'and I needed to put food on the table for my family.

'Gordon is a maverick giver,' Bird goes on. 'Who else would have given a 45-year-old social failure a chance?' But the more Bird spoke to homeless people and to the police, the more he became convinced the *Big Issue* could work. 'I suddenly realised this wasn't charity and it could actually do something. I wrote a report in six weeks.' He laughs. 'Most of it was b******s.'

In the early days, Bird employed friends, family and some people he had met in a cafe. 'Most of them were people who knew nothing about papers.' The first issue he describes as like 'a bad student magazine', and the first person he met selling the fledgling *Big Issue* was rolling drunk.

'It was awful,' Bird, now 63, says. 'He said I was exploiting the homeless. I said, "Well, why are you doing it then?" And he said, "I'm doing it for my baby in Liverpool." I said, "Well, it sounds like you need me and I need you then."'

Bird shakes his head. 'There's never been any love lost between me and the homeless. People knew I was ex-homeless, an ex-offender. They'd say, "You've gone to the other side." They abused me because they had to pay for the paper. It was invigorating.'

That first Christmas, the *Big Issue* held a party for its vendors in the crypt of St-Martin-in-the-Fields. 'My brother brought in 400 cans of Special Brew,' Bird remembers. 'It was the unbelievably maddest office Christmas party I've ever been to. It took seven hours to get everyone out of the crypt. St Martin's said we were an embarrassment to anybody who wanted to help the homeless.'

The magazine was soon losing £25,000 a month of Body Shop Foundation money. 'Gordon put a gun to my head,' Bird recalls. 'He said, you've got three months to break even. I cut jobs, put the price to the vendor up, moved it from monthly to fortnightly and told everyone to work twice as hard. We went from losing £25,000 a month to £1,000 profit.'

Today there is also the Big Issue Foundation, which gives support and advice to vendors; versions of the magazine are sold from Australia to Japan, South Africa to Namibia. And its founders are still pushing the original model forward with Big Issue Invest – a new social enterprise investment fund that finances social businesses.

At its head office in Vauxhall, south London, an editorial meeting is discussing the magazine's sought-after interview with Leona Lewis, ethical food, and the shocking death of a vendor in Regent Street, impaled on glass from a shop window. The story has been reported nationally in lurid detail, but reporters here are determined to investigate the story properly.

'Our whole mission is about the vendor,' says the editor, Charles Howgego. 'We have to see the world through the eyes of someone who's got nowhere to sleep at night. Everybody on the editorial team knows vendors personally, and everyone knows what they go through. That's a very strong motivation.'

A few years ago, the *Guardian* ran a story by a former *Big Issue* deputy editor, Adam MacQueen, suggesting

Bird might now be its 'biggest problem' – but 38-year-old Howgego says he remains 'the soul of the organisation'.

Below the editorial floor is the distribution office, where vendors collect magazines and drop in for advice and support. It often receives complaints about illegal vendors who aren't employed by the organisation, but are begging with a single copy. Genuine vendors sign up to a code of conduct, and are easily recognisable with a badge clearly on display.

'People sometimes complain that they've seen a person selling who isn't homeless,' says Paul Joseph, the distribution manager. 'But we don't sack vulnerable people just because they've become housed. Exiting homelessness can be a long, drawn-out process.'

'I haven't been in jail since I started selling the paper'

In Covent Garden, Billie Bickley introduces one of her star customers, Nick Paris, 49, who works nearby in investment sales and has just done the *Big Issue*'s London to Paris bike ride. 'He made £5k, the top fundraiser,' she says. 'He's invested in me, he says.'

Bickley started selling the *Big Issue* a decade ago. 'I haven't been in jail since,' she says. 'Not once. After 96 convictions, it's been my life saver.'

18 years on, though, Bird wishes the *Big Issue* was no longer necessary. 'There has been an improvement,' he says. 'This Government chose to take responsibility for street homelessness. But the problem now is a different one – institutionalised homelessness.

'Now we need to dismantle homelessness. You can't just take a really f****d-up person and say, here's a sink and phone and a place to watch TV, and a couple of hours counselling a week. It's like trying to do an organ transplant with a knife and fork. You need more than knives, forks, walls and windows to sort out the damage done to people on the streets.'

Yesterday, Bickley was one of four vendors chosen to visit Downing Street to mark the *Big Issue*'s 18th birthday. She sold a copy to Gordon Brown within minutes. This summer, she has also been to the Big Chill to sell the festival programme on site. 'I don't know if I'd go again,' she says, packing up for the day. 'The toilets were filthy.'

Now that she's living in a proper home with her partner Aden, a cleaner at the hostel she had been staying in, Bickley says she has become a cleanliness freak, constantly cleaning and tidying. She grins lopsidedly at her dog. 'House proud, you could say.'

18 September 2009

© Guardian News and Media Limited 2009

The Big Issue – how we work

The *Big Issue* exists to offer homeless and vulnerably housed people the opportunity to earn a legitimate income by selling a magazine to the general public. We believe in offering 'a hand up, not a hand out' and in enabling individuals to take control of their lives.

In order to become a *Big Issue* vendor an individual must prove that they are homeless or vulnerably housed, undergo an induction process and sign up to the code of conduct. Once they have done so they are allocated a fixed pitch and issued with five free copies of the magazine (or ten in London). Once they have sold these magazines they can purchase further copies, which they buy for 85p and sell for £1.70, thereby making 85p per copy.

Vendors are not employed by the *Big Issue*, and we do not reimburse them for magazines which they fail to sell, hence each individual must manage their sales and finances carefully. These skills, along with the confidence and self-esteem they build through selling the magazine, are crucial in helping homeless people reintegrate into mainstream society.

And we don't stop there. We recognise that earning an income is first step on the journey away from homelessness, and that a variety of issues may have contributed to an individual becoming homeless. The Big Issue Foundation, a registered charity, exists to link vendors with the vital support and services which will help them address these issues and fulfil their potential.

We work exclusively with vendors, offering advice and referrals in four keys areas: housing, health, financial independence and aspirations. Our definition of success is people making positive life changes.

The Foundation is committed to providing this crucial support in all the areas in which the magazine is sold. We rely almost entirely on voluntary donations and receive minimum support from statutory and Government funding, hence the need for your support. Without the generosity of individual donors and charitable trusts we simply would not exist.

⇨ The above information is reprinted with kind permission from the *Big Issue*. Visit www.bigissue.com for more information.

© The Big Issue 2010

⇨ Many people only associate homelessness with sleeping on the streets, but this conceals the range and scale of the problem. The reality is that the vast majority of homeless people are families or single people who are not 'sleeping rough'. (page 1)

⇨ Many households who approach local authorities as homeless do not fit statutory homelessness criteria and therefore do not qualify for rehousing, even though they may have a serious housing need. For example, the local authority will not have a duty to house a family with children if they are deemed intentionally homeless. There will also be no duty owed to an asylum seeker as they will not be eligible due to their immigration status. (page 2)

⇨ The number of households living in temporary accommodation reached its most recent high point in 2004, with 101,300 falling into this category. (page 3)

⇨ Rough sleepers include those people sleeping, or bedded down, in the open air (such as on the streets, or in doorways, parks or bus shelters), and people in buildings or other places not designed for habitation (such as barns, sheds, car parks, cars, derelict boats, or stations). Rough sleeping is currently at its lowest recorded level. (page 4)

⇨ 23% of people accepted as homeless in the last quarter of 2008 gave parents being unwilling or unable to accommodate them as the primary reason for the loss of a secure home. (page 5)

⇨ Recent data from homelessness day centres and accommodation projects across England shows that, on average, 18% of clients were prison leavers, 14% were care leavers and 6% were ex-service personnel. (page 6)

⇨ Homelessness acceptances peaked in 2003/2004, and since then are 71 per cent lower. (page 8)

⇨ Mental health needs combined with substance misuse issues ('dual diagnosis') are extremely common among the homeless population. (page 10)

⇨ In St Mungos hostels in 2007, it was found that: 32% of residents had an alcohol dependency; 63% had a drugs problem; 49% had a mental health problem, and 43% had a physical illness. (page 12)

⇨ One drink- or drug-addicted homeless person is admitted to hospital every three hours, putting a severe strain on the National Health Service, new figures show. (page 13)

⇨ A major report in 2009 exposed the worsening crisis amongst refused asylum seekers in the UK, as it reveals that more than a third have been destitute for over a year, with two out of every three of those homeless originating from some of the most troubled countries in the world. (page 14)

⇨ 23% of people in the 25–34 age group were concerned about the possibility of being forced to leave their home during the next 12 months due to falling behind on mortgage or rent payments. (page 18)

⇨ 44% of people surveyed agreed strongly that the Government should be doing more to help prevent those at risk from losing their home. (page 19)

⇨ The breakdown of family relationships has been identified as the main cause of homelessness, often following years of family conflict and some violent and abusive situations. In a survey of 50 families affected by youth homelessness, 72% of parents believe that extra help could prevent family breakdown. (page 21)

⇨ It is very difficult to have a full picture of the numbers of young people who are homeless. Often single homeless young people exist out of sight due to 'sofa surfing' or staying with friends, or living in squats or hostels. Not all homeless young people approach their local council for help. (page 23)

⇨ An estimated 100,000 children and young people run away each year in the UK for a wide variety of reasons such as physical, sexual, verbal or emotional abuse, neglect and peer pressure. (page 25)

⇨ According to Barnardo's, there are 52,250 homeless families in London and another 20,000 throughout the UK. Of these, 73% involve minors, putting the overall estimate of homeless children at more than 130,000. (page 29)

⇨ With an employment rate of 15%, homeless people are five times less likely than the wider population to be in employment. However, the vast majority of homeless people want to work either now (77%) or in the future (97%). (page 33)

⇨ The *Big Issue* is not a charity handout; vendors buy the magazine for 85p and sell it for £1.70. (page 39)

Begging

A beggar is someone who makes money by asking for donations from passers-by. Although begging and homelessness are inextricably linked, not all rough sleepers beg or vice versa.

The Big Issue

A weekly magazine sold by homeless people in the UK. Launched in 1995, the money made from magazine sales is used to benefit homeless people.

Hidden homelessness

In addition to those people recognised as statutory homeless there are also a large number of homeless single adults, or couples without dependent children, who meet the legal definition of homelessness but not the criteria for priority need. In many cases they will not even apply for official recognition, knowing they do not meet the criteria. Statistics provided by the Government will therefore not include all people in the country who actually meet the definition of homelessness. As a result, this group is often referred to as the hidden homeless.

Homeless households

A family or individual who has applied for local authority housing support and been judged to be homeless.

Homelessness

The law defines somebody as being homeless if they do not have a legal right to occupy any accommodation, or if their accommodation is unsuitable to live in. This can cover a wide range of circumstances, including, but not restricted to, the following:

⇨ having no accommodation at all;

⇨ having accommodation that is not reasonable to live in, even in the short-term (e.g. because of violence or health reasons);

⇨ having a legal right to accommodation that for some reason you cannot access (e.g. if you have been illegally evicted);

⇨ living in accommodation you have no legal right to occupy (e.g. living in a squat or temporarily staying with friends).

Hostels and nightshelters

Hostels and nightshelters provide housing for people sleeping on the streets.

Priority need

Under homelessness legislation, certain categories of household are considered to have priority need for accommodation. Priority need applies to all households that contain a pregnant woman or are responsible for dependent children; to some households made up of a 16- to 17-year-old or a care leaver aged 18 to 21; or where someone is vulnerable, e.g. because of old age, health problems; or by being in prison, care or the Forces.

Rough sleeping

A rough sleeper is a homeless person who is literally 'roofless' and lives predominantly on the streets. The total number of people found rough sleeping by local authority street counts has fallen by nearly three-quarters – from 1,850 in 1998 to 464 in 2009.

Single homeless

This term refers to homeless individuals or couples without dependants.

Statutory homelessness

In England, people who are accepted by local authorities as being officially homeless, and who are deemed to have a priority need, are referred to as statutory homeless. Local authorities have a duty to accommodate people who are statutory homeless, as long as they also have a local connection and have not made themselves homeless intentionally. In England in 2007–08, local authorities made 130,840 decisions on applications for housing assistance under the Housing Act 1996. Of these decisions, 63,170 resulted in the authority accepting the applicant as being statutory homeless.

Street homelessness

Often confused with rough sleeping, street homelessness is actually a much wider term, also taking into account the street lifestyles of some people who may not actually sleep on the streets.

Additional Resources

Other Issues *titles*

If you are interested in researching further some of the issues raised in *The Homeless Population,* you may like to read the following titles in the *Issues* series:

⇨ Vol. 183 *Work and Employment* (ISBN 978 1 86168 524 7)

⇨ Vol. 181 *The Housing Issue* (ISBN 978 1 86168 505 6)

⇨ Vol. 180 *Money and Finances* (ISBN 978 1 86168 504 9)

⇨ Vol. 177 *Crime in the UK* (ISBN 978 1 86168 501 8)

⇨ Vol. 160 *Poverty and Exclusion* (ISBN 978 1 86168 453 0)

For a complete list of available *Issues* titles, please visit our website: www.independence.co.uk/shop

Useful organisations

You may find the websites of the following organisations useful for further research:

⇨ **Centrepoint:** www.centrepoint.org.uk

⇨ **Crisis:** www.crisis.org.uk

⇨ **Department for Communities and Local Government:** www.communities.gov.uk

⇨ **Homeless Link:** www.homeless.org.uk

⇨ **Inside Housing:** www.insidehousing.co.uk

⇨ **OSW:** www.osw.org.uk

⇨ **The Railway Children:** www.railwaychildren.org.uk

⇨ **Refugee Action:** www.refugee-action.org.uk

⇨ **Shelter:** www.shelter.org.uk

⇨ **St Mungo's:** www.mungos.org

⇨ **Thames Reach:** www.thamesreach.org.uk

For more book information, visit our website...

www.independence.co.uk

Information available online includes:

✓ Detailed descriptions of titles

✓ Tables of contents

✓ Facts and figures

✓ Online ordering facilities

✓ Log-in page for Issues Online (an Internet resource available free to Firm Order Issues subscribers – ask your librarian to find out if this service is available to you)

ACKNOWLEDGEMENTS

The publisher is grateful for permission to reproduce the following material.

While every care has been taken to trace and acknowledge copyright, the publisher tenders its apology for any accidental infringement or where copyright has proved untraceable. The publisher would be pleased to come to a suitable arrangement in any such case with the rightful owner.

Chapter One: Homelessness Issues

What is homelessness?, © Shelter, *Homelessness statistics,* © OSW, *Causes and effects of homelessness,* © OSW, *Transitions/leaving an institution,* © Crisis, *Sofa surfing,* © need2know, *Homelessness trends,* © Crown copyright is reproduced with the permission of Her Majesty's Stationery Office, *Happiness matters,* © St Mungos, *Figures from* Rough sleeping in a recession: summary report *[graphs],* © Ipsos MORI, *Homelessness – it makes you sick,* © St Mungo's, *Drunk and overdosing homeless people put strain on NHS,* © Telegraph Media Group Limited 2010, *Asylum seeker suffering hits new depths as destitution lasts for years,* © Joseph Rowntree Charitable Trust, *Destitution: asylum's untold story,* © Refugee Action, *Rough Sleeping,* © Homeless Link, *Physical health problems suffered by homeless people [graph],* © St Mungo's, *Figures from* Rough sleeping in a recession - topline results *[graph],* © Ipsos MORI, *Life on the streets,* © The Scotsman, *Figures from* Rough sleeping in a recession: summary report *[graphs],* © Ipsos MORI.

Chapter Two: Youth Homelessness

Young people and homelessness, © YMCA, *Emily's Life,* © Centrepoint, *Hidden homelessness,* © Centrepoint, *Youth homelessness,* © Crown copyright is reproduced with the permission of Her Majesty's Stationery Office, *Young runaways,* © Crown copyright is reproduced with the permission of Her Majesty's Stationery Office, *Family breakdown to blame for youth homelessness,* © Inside Housing, *Homeless acceptances in priority need by need category [graph],* © Crown copyright is reproduced with the permission of Her Majesty's Stationery Office, *Off the radar,* © The Railway Children, *No place like home,* © Guardian News and Media Limited 2009.

Chapter Three: Homelessness Solutions

Work and skills, © Crisis, *Homelessness prevention,* © Shelter, *Why giving to those who beg does more harm than good,* © Thames Reach, *The Big Issue celebrates its 18th birthday,* © Guardian News and Media Limited 2009, *The Big Issue – how we work,* © The Big Issue 2010.

Illustrations

Pages 1, 7, 16, 37: Simon Kneebone; pages 2a, 2b, 12, 35: Don Hatcher; pages 3, 14, 23, 38: Angelo Madrid; pages 4, 20: Bev Aisbett.

Cover photography

Left: © madmick99. Centre: © J Cash. Right: © John Evans.

Additional acknowledgements

With thanks to the Independence team: Mary Chapman, Sandra Dennis and Jan Sunderland.

Lisa Firth
Cambridge
May, 2010